Guideposts

the joys of Christmas 2025

*Rejoice in the Lord always:
and again I say, Rejoice.*

PHILIPPIANS 4:4 (KJV)

Guideposts is a nonprofit organization that promotes faith, hope and prayer in people's lives. Whether through our apps, communities, websites or publications, we inspire our audiences, bring them together, comfort, uplift, entertain and guide them. To learn more, visit **guideposts.org/about** or **guidepostsfoundation.org**.

contents

FEATURES

- **6** POEMS
  "A CHRISTMAS CAROL"
  "CHRISTMAS BELLS"
- **7** LETTER FROM THE EDITOR
- **8** ADVENT CALENDAR
- **10** 'TIS THE SEASON
- **11** THE CHRISTMAS STORY
- **16** A PREVIEW FROM *WALKING IN GRACE 2026*
  by Penney Schwab
- **34** MYSTERIOUS WAYS
  by Amy Brady ★
- **52** WHAT PRAYER CAN DO
  by Jeannie Hughes
- **83** POEM
  "FROM HEAVEN ABOVE TO EARTH I COME"

the joy of christmas wishes

- **18** RESCUING CARMELLA
  by Dana Polito-Corry ★
- **22** OUR QUIRKY FAMILY TREE
  by Kristy Dewberry
- **25** WARM WINTER WINK
  by Laura Kaye
- **26** MOM'S CHRISTMAS WISH
  by Mary Whitney ★
- **29** TEAMWORK!
  by Anne Munson
- **32** STAMPED WITH LOVE
  by Richard H. Schneider ★

the joy of god's grace

- **36** COMFORT AND JOY
  by Diane Stark
- **40** BEST GIFT EVER
  by Meg Belviso
- **42** DESTINATION CHRISTMAS!
  by Gloria Joyce
- **45** SMUDGES ON THE WINDOW
  by Diane Kalusniak
- **46** SADIE, YOU ARE LOVED
  by Lynne Hartke
- **49** RUTH'S REINDEER CARD
  by Meadow Rue Merrill

the joy of nostalgia

- **54** AFTER HOURS
  by Jennie Ivey
- **57** SHARED MEMORIES
  by Nicki Cooper
- **60** I REMEMBER...
  by Norman Vincent Peale
- **64** GUESTS AT THE BARN
  by Isabel Wolseley Torrey ★
- **67** JUST A PEEK
  by Rose Ross Zediker
- **68** VISITORS TO THE PARSONAGE
  by Daniel Schantz
- **71** ALL THE LOVING REASONS
  by Aline Alexander Newman

the joy of cranberries

- **74** KITCHEN TIME
  by Whitney Miller
- **77** BOOK CLUB RECS
  by Cita Smith
- **78** A BOWL OF BRIGHTNESS
  by Al Roker
- **80** SLICE OF LIFE
  by Jessica Merchant

★ Enjoy these Reader Favorites!

11

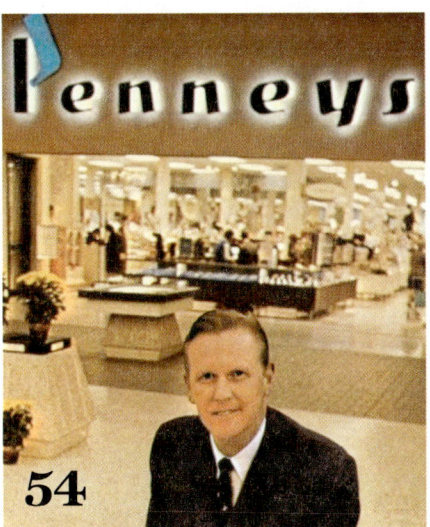

42

54

Guideposts

PRESIDENT & CEO John Temple
EDITOR-IN-CHIEF Edward Grinnan
VICE PRESIDENT, CONTENT Ansley Roan
LEAD EDITOR Colleen Hughes
CREATIVE DIRECTOR Kayo Der Sarkissian
MAGAZINE Meg Belviso, Kevin Eans, Kimberly Elkins, Celia M. Gibbons, Lisa Guernsey, Beth Meyer, Evan Miller, Andrew Nahem, Nikki Notare, Nicole White, Amy Wong
DIGITAL Sabra Ciancanelli, Rachel Engdall, Matthew Fogle, Matt Honkonen, Kaylin Kaupish, Ashley Lateef, Lauren Leakey, Brett Leveridge, Carolyn Mandarano, Carolina Pichardo, Stephanie Reeves, Mike Rotella, Tay Schmidt, Daisy T. Urgiles, Grace Wyckoff
BOOK Morgan Beard, Valentina Chiofalo, Sabrina Diaz, Amanda Ericson, Jane Haertel, Joanna Kennedy, Rose Tussing

CREATIVE CONSULTANT Kathi Rota
COPY & PRODUCTION CONSULTANT Diane Sinitsky
CONTRIBUTING EDITORS Rick Hamlin, Celeste McCauley, Ginger Rue
SENIOR VICE PRESIDENTS Kelly Mangold, Zuri Rice, David Teitler
VICE PRESIDENTS James Asselmeyer, Julian Lama, Kathleen Miller, Nisarg Parikh, Ty'Ann Williams

Guideposts' *The Joys of Christmas* is published by Guideposts, 100 Reserve Road, Suite E200, Danbury, CT 06810. Canadian GST #893989236. Copyright © 2025 by Guideposts, all rights reserved. Volume 17, No. 1. Issue Date: December 2025. Printed in U.S.A. Send address changes to Guideposts, P.O. Box 5827, Tipton, IA 52772-0547. Canada Post: Send address changes to Guideposts, P.O. Box 1051, Fort Erie, ON L2A 6C7.
ISBN 978-1-965859-42-1 (Print), ISBN 978-1-965859-67-4 (ePub)

The Joys of Christmas makes a wonderful gift! Order extra copies at guideposts.org/joc.

COVER: ILLUSTRATION BY SONIA PULIDO; THIS PAGE, LEFT: COURTESY JENNIE IVEY; RIGHT: COURTESY GLORIA JOYCE

A Christmas Carol

There's a song in the air!
There's a star in the sky!
There's a mother's deep prayer
And a baby's low cry!
    And the star rains its fire while the beautiful sing,
    For the manger of Bethlehem cradles a king.

—JOSIAH GILBERT HOLLAND

Christmas Bells

I heard the bells on Christmas Day
Their old, familiar carols play,
    And wild and sweet
    The words repeat
Of peace on earth, good-will to men!

—HENRY WADSWORTH LONGFELLOW

LETTER FROM THE EDITOR

Remembering...

MY MOTHER HATED when I called her sentimental, but she was. I'd catch her misty-eyed, all curled up on the couch, watching *The Waltons* holiday special, *The Homecoming: A Christmas Story,* and whisper, "Busted."

I always look forward to what *The Joys of Christmas* story themes will be. I was excited to see a "Nostalgia" section this year. It's been a while since we've done this cozy topic. I guess I was nostalgic for nostalgia. Which brings me back to Mom.

Why would a struggling family like the Waltons summon such warm feelings in her? Mom and her five siblings came of age in the Depression, when as much as a quarter of the country was out of work. I think what Mom recalled was how her family counted on each other and their faith to get through such hard times. I'm sure those were some of her best Christmases when they barely had anything but each other, and it was all they needed.

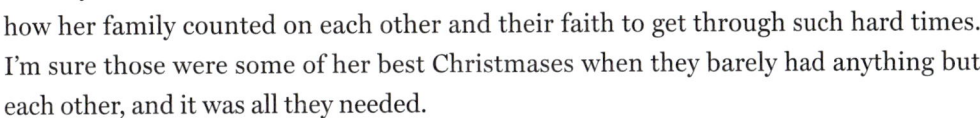

Nostalgia sometimes gets a bad rap for being escapist. But nostalgia arises from the power of memory. That certain moments from our past glow in our memories, especially at Christmas, is a blessing. I confess I've inherited my mother's nostalgia, and I have a Christmas moment of my own to prove it.

I spent the year after college wandering through the Caribbean and South America and not doing a very good job of staying in touch. On a late November morning, I was picking my way through a remote marketplace high in the Ecuadorean Andes. Indigenous people traveled many rugged miles to display their wares, as they had for centuries. My ragtag group had come by horseback. A companion happened to mention that the Christmas season must be in full swing back in the States, and all at once, with a startling pang, I saw the decorated windows at Hudson's flagship department store, the poinsettias on the altar at St. Owen's and the Nativity that was always up the week after Thanksgiving in my parents' living room. Suddenly, urgently, I realized I had to turn around that very day and make my way home for Christmas. That memory has stayed with me for all these years with amazing clarity.

What lasting memory does Christmas hold for you? Share it this season with your family and loved ones. I bet you're not the only one who's feeling nostalgic.

Edward

EDWARD GRINNAN
Editor-in-Chief, Guideposts

2025 Advent

SUNDAY	MONDAY	TUESDAY
Nov 30 — FIRST SUNDAY — *"Thy word is a lamp to my feet and a light to my path."* —PSALM 119:105	**Dec 1** — Remember, adventure and Advent have the same Latin root.	**2** — Google "DIY Advent wreaths" and make one that speaks to you.
Dec 7 — SECOND SUNDAY — *"Do not let your hearts be troubled and do not be afraid."* —JOHN 14:27	**8** — Put your worries in the empty crèche.	**9** — Relax! You are so loved!
Dec 14 — THIRD SUNDAY — *"Let your gentleness be evident to all."* —PHILIPPIANS 4:5	**15** — It's a perfect day to forgive someone.	**16** — Fill your bird feeders (or hang one).
Dec 21 — FOURTH SUNDAY — *"To us a child is born."* —ISAIAH 9:6	**22** — Listen to the young people in your life. Out of the mouths of babes…	**23** — Find a translation of the French carol "Bring a Torch, Jeanette, Isabella."

Calendar

WEDNESDAY	THURSDAY	FRIDAY	SATURDAY
3 Reach out to someone you've been thinking about.	**4** Surprise your mail carrier with a thank-you.	**5** God gave you smile lines for a reason.	**6** Bake cookies for a family at church.
10 Pray for peace on earth and in your heart.	**11** Check on a friend or neighbor who lives alone.	**12** Fall asleep counting the shepherds' sheep. (Yes, those shepherds.)	**13** Patience, patience, patience.
17 Put your feet up for a Christmas movie.	**18** Be a secret Santa to a family in need.	**19** Remember the strays this season.	**20** Shop local, love global!
24 If there isn't a bright star in the sky, imagine one.	**25** *Merry Christmas to all!*		

'Tis the Season

"Joy energizes. Joy lifts. Joy engages you with the giver. Joy casts your visions off of yourself and onto Him. Is it any wonder we sing 'Joy to the World!' at Christmastime?"
—WANDA E. BRUNSTETTER, AUTHOR

"For it is good to be children sometimes, and never better than at Christmas, when its mighty Founder was a child himself."
—FROM *A CHRISTMAS CAROL* BY CHARLES DICKENS

"Christmas in Bethlehem... a cold, clear night made brilliant by a glorious star, the smell of incense, shepherds and wise men falling to their knees in adoration of the sweet baby, the incarnation of perfect love."
—LUCINDA FRANKS, JOURNALIST

"No matter what your Christmas season will look like—whether it's exactly what you imagined or the exact opposite of your holiday dreams—bring it all to Jesus anyway. He's with you in the mess, and He's making your messy moments into holy ones."
—ASHERITAH CIUCIU, WRITER, ON LEARNING TO APPRECIATE AN "IMPERFECT" CHRISTMAS

"It's not about presents, but it is about your presence. Therein lies the spirit of the holiday season!"
—JULIEANNE O'CONNOR, AUTHOR AND SPEAKER

"Joy is not the absence of sadness or the presence of the spectacular. It's the undercurrent of understanding God's goodness in every season."
—TAUREN WELLS, SINGER AND PASTOR

> **"Things that are warm at Christmas... Mittens from Grandma. Houses after sledding. Hugs and kisses. Hearts for each other."**
> —MARJORIE HOLMES, AUTHOR

the Christmas Story

Gather round for our read-aloud feature

GOD SENT THE angel Gabriel to Nazareth, a city in Galilee, to a virgin who was engaged to a man named Joseph, a descendant of David's house. The virgin's name was Mary. When the angel came to her, he said, "Rejoice, favored one! The Lord is with you!" She was confused by these words and wondered what kind of greeting this might be. The angel said, "Don't be afraid, Mary. God is honoring you. Look! You will conceive and give birth to a son, and you will name him Jesus." —LUKE 1:26–31

ILLUSTRATIONS BY AMALIA RESTREPO
"The thing that really matters to me, as an artist, is the ability to connect with humanity," says Colombian illustrator and architect Amalia Restrepo. "I try to evoke dreams, nostalgia and a sense of familiarity, similar to the sense of returning to your childhood home." Her work has been exhibited and won awards around the world, and for us here, she has brought the Christmas story to life.

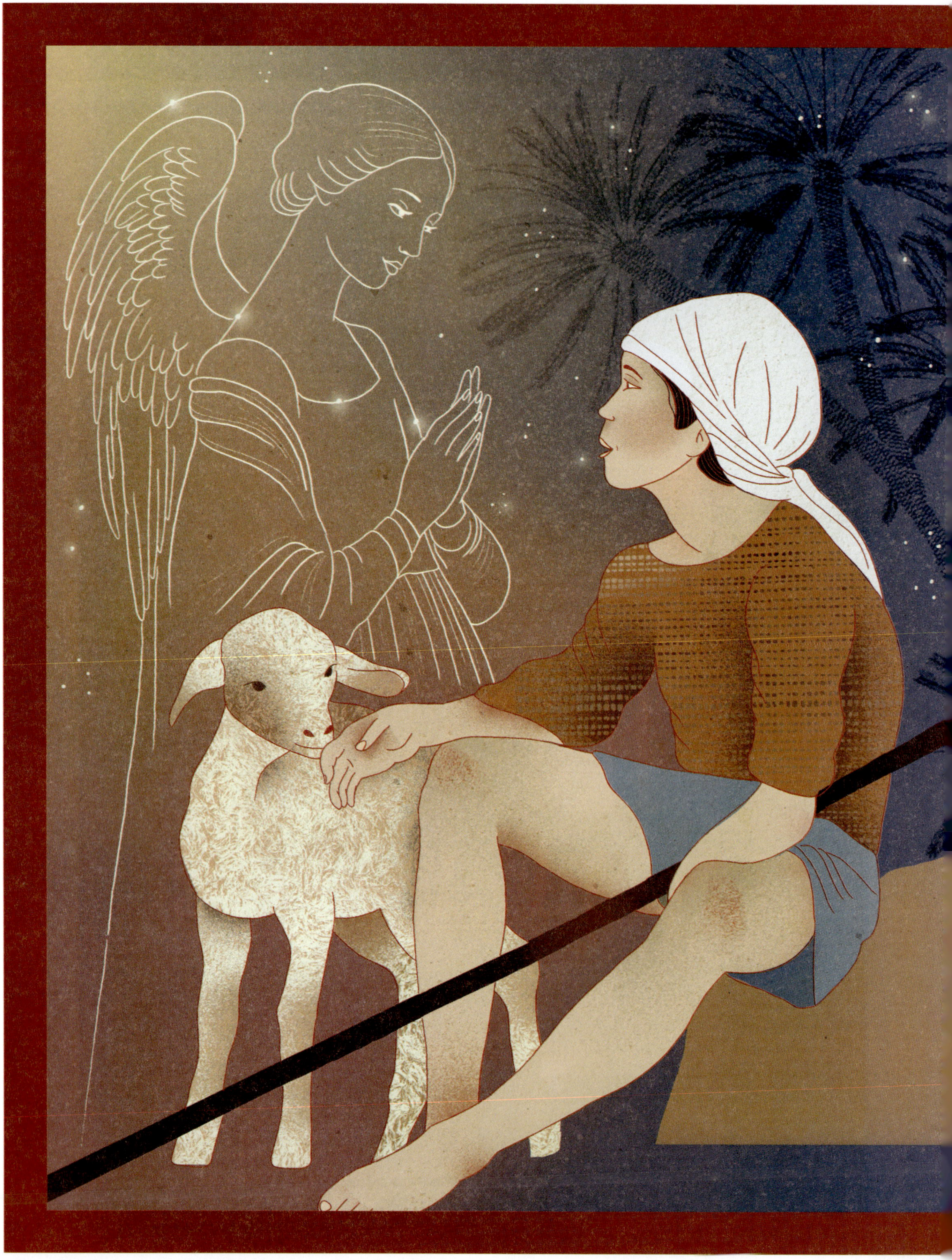

After Jesus was born in Bethlehem in the territory of Judea during the rule of King Herod, magi came from the east to Jerusalem. They asked, "Where is the newborn king of the Jews? We've seen his star in the east, and we've come to honor him." When King Herod heard this, he was troubled, and everyone in Jerusalem was troubled with him. Then Herod secretly called for the magi and found out from them the time when the star had first appeared. He sent them to Bethlehem, saying, "Go and search carefully for the child." —Matthew 2:1–3, 7–8

Nearby shepherds were living in the fields, guarding their sheep at night. The Lord's angel stood before them, the Lord's glory shone around them, and they were terrified. The angel said, "Don't be afraid! Look! I bring good news to you—wonderful, joyous news for all people. Your savior is born today in David's city. He is Christ the Lord. This is a sign for you: you will find a newborn baby wrapped snugly and lying in a manger."
—Luke 2:8–12

IN THOSE DAYS Caesar Augustus declared that everyone throughout the empire should be enrolled in the tax lists. Since Joseph belonged to David's house and family line, he went up from the city of Nazareth in Galilee to David's city, called Bethlehem, in Judea. He went to be enrolled together with Mary, who was promised to him in marriage and who was pregnant. While they were there, the time came for Mary to have her baby. She gave birth to her firstborn child, a son, wrapped him snugly, and laid him in a manger. —LUKE 2:1, 4–7

MARY COMMITTED these things to memory and considered them carefully. The shepherds returned home, glorifying and praising God for all they had heard and seen. Everything happened just as they had been told.
—LUKE 2:19–20

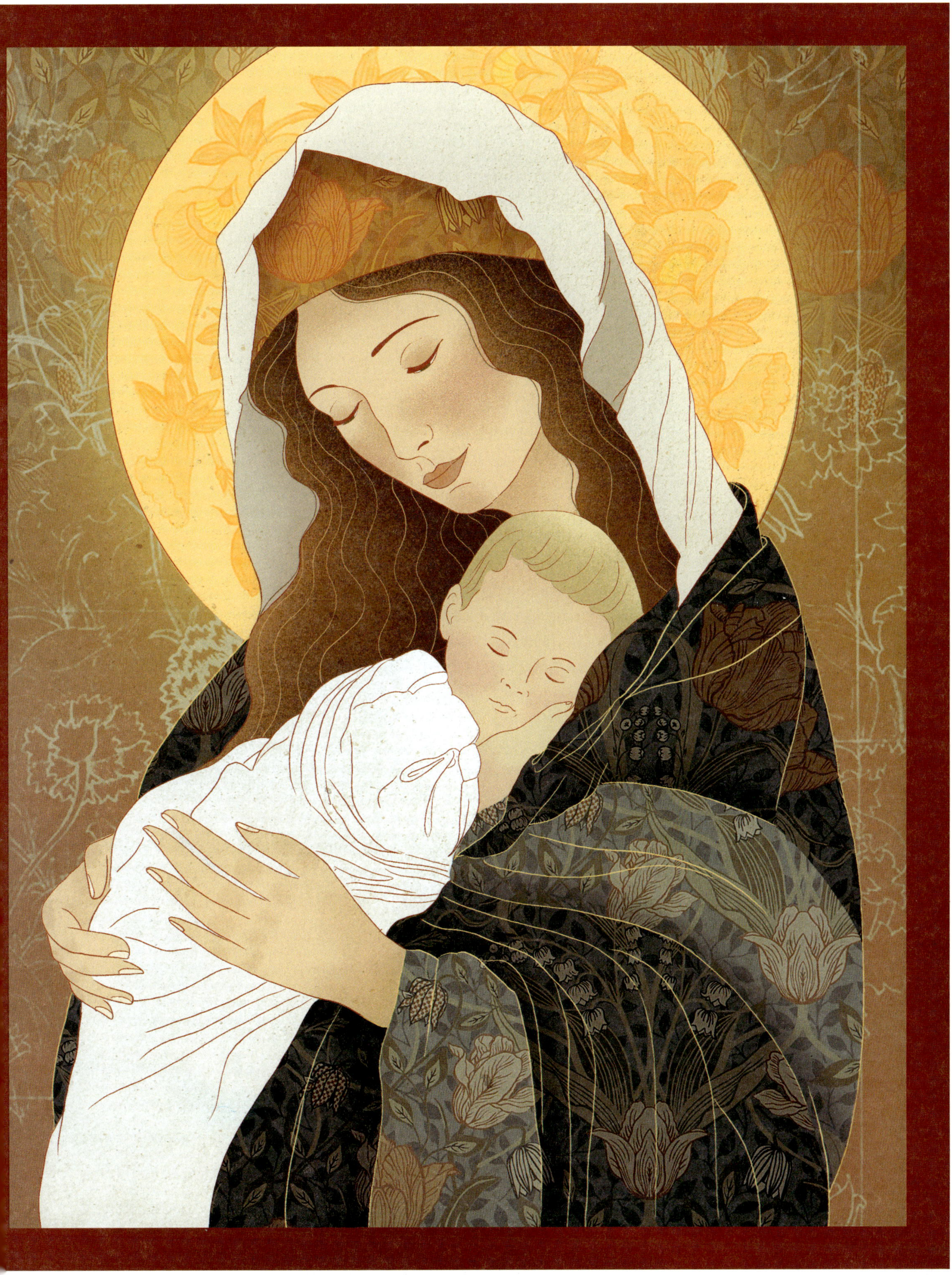

A PREVIEW FROM THE 2026 EDITION

WALKING IN GRACE

So then, brothers and sisters, stand firm and hold fast to the teachings we passed on to you, whether by word of mouth or by letter.
2 THESSALONIANS 2:15 (NIV)

I DECIDED NOT to decorate for Christmas, now that my husband, Don, was gone. I felt a bit guilty. Don had loved every display and every ornament we owned, but getting them out by myself would take several hours and multiple trips to the basement. I wasn't up to it.

A couple of weeks into December, I did manage to put up a quilted wall hanging, a handmade gift from my dear friend Martha, over the fireplace. The panels portrayed the birth of Christ in vivid shades of blue, green and gold. I loved to sit and admire it. The piece seemed to want company, so I put a needlepoint picture of the Holy Family in the dining room. I rummaged around in the basement.

One thing led to another, and soon the house was decorated. Four Nativity sets were displayed in the dining room. The pewter one with exquisite figurines was a gift from Don. Another was handmade from corn husks; I'd spent my Christmas money to buy it from a mission agency 40 years earlier. The Nativity with vividly painted tin figures was from Mexico. A stable and its rough-cut wooden figures had been arranged and rearranged often by my young children. A bowl of pine cones adorned the living room coffee table. I even set out the basket of coasters that were handmade from old Christmas cards. They were a bit tacky, but I liked them.

When I lit the candles on the Advent wreath and saw my angel collection reflected in the light, I was thankful I'd kept alive the holiday tradition Don loved. Every decoration brought precious memories that helped me move toward Christmas Day with joy.

Thank you, Jesus, for treasures and traditions that draw me closer to you.
—PENNEY SCHWAB

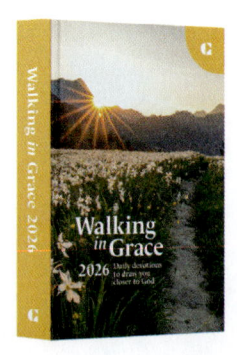

Walking in Grace is our most popular devotional book. To order the 2026 edition, visit **guideposts.org/wig**; write to Guideposts, P.O. Box 5828, Tipton, IA 52772; or call (800) 932-2145. It is available in a hardcover edition for $16.95 or in a softcover large-print edition for $17.95, plus shipping and processing.

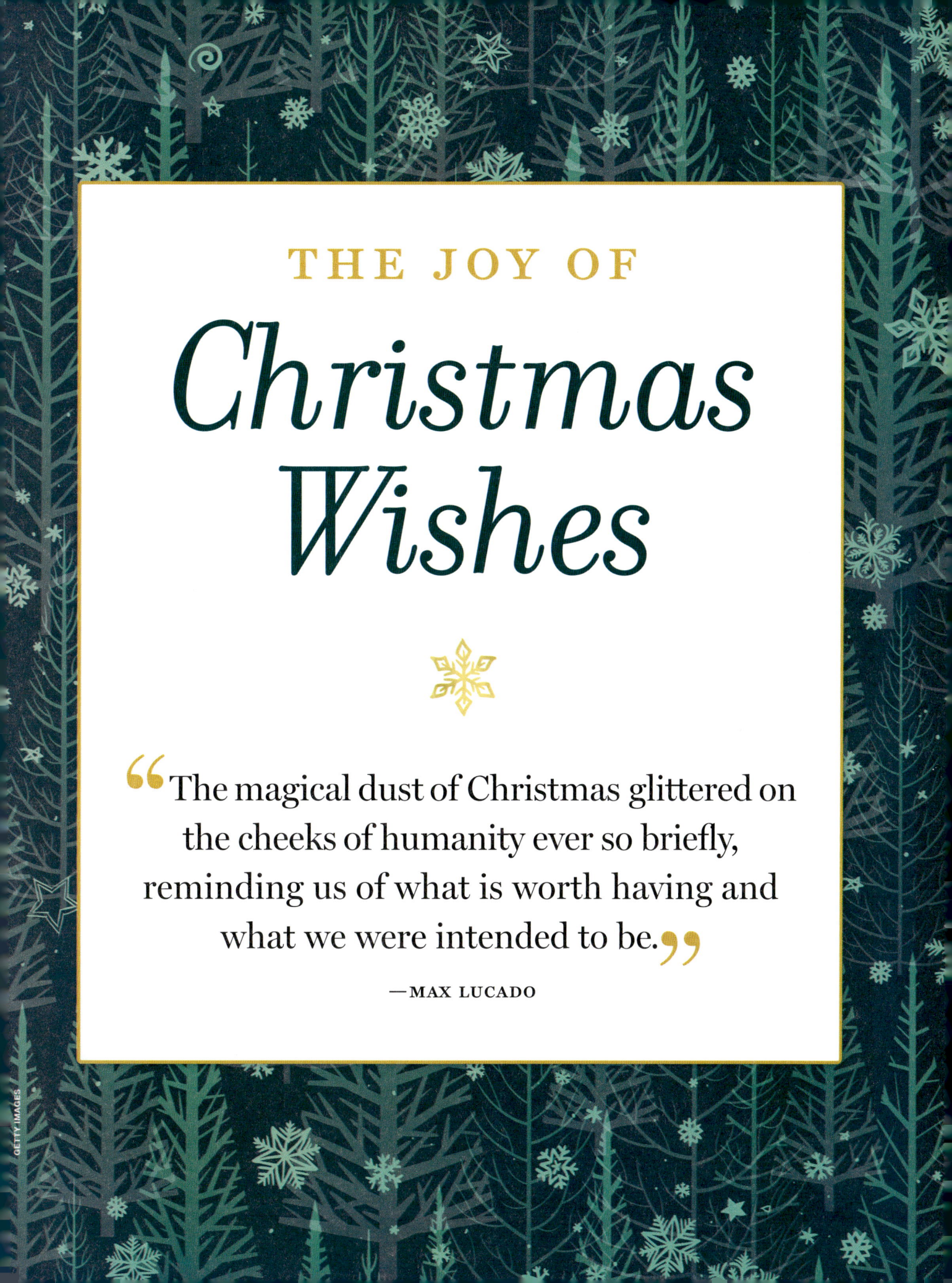

THE JOY OF
Christmas Wishes

❄

"The magical dust of Christmas glittered on the cheeks of humanity ever so briefly, reminding us of what is worth having and what we were intended to be."

—MAX LUCADO

THE JOY OF *christmas wishes*

Rescuing Carmella

My daughters had just one thing on their Christmas list—a dog as special as they are

by **DANA POLITO-CORRY,** Wayne, New Jersey

READER FAVORITE

THE GIRLS NEVER asked for much for Christmas. We were in the car; I was driving them to their weekly appointment with the therapist. I could see them in the back seat in the rearview mirror. "Mom," Tianna said, "I want a dog for Christmas."

Tianna didn't speak much. Like her 10-year-old twin sister, Gianna, she lives with multiple disabilities. Both of them are legally blind, Gianna is autistic and Tianna has selective mutism. Getting a word out of her could be difficult. She certainly never spoke to strangers, and sometimes, I worried, she wouldn't even tell me what was on her mind. That's why I had to pay attention to this dog request.

"But we already have four dogs," I said. A couple of years back, the girls' neurologist had suggested that a dog might help them with their communication skills and give them someone to bond with. We'd started out small with Skater, a mini fox terrier and Chihuahua mix, and the menagerie had grown from there to include two more Chihuahuas and a 100-pound pit bull named Chaos.

That name proved accurate. Our household was usually in a chaos of water bowls, food dishes, leashes, crates, collars, treats, chew toys and balls. We had covers on all

WELL MATCHED
Tianna (left) and Gianna with their favorite girl, Carmella

the joys of Christmas 19

the furniture, paw prints were everywhere and nearly every unprotected surface had tooth marks. But the doctor was right. It was worth it. The dogs drew the girls out, gave them added responsibilities, received their hugs and leaped to their call. Somehow everybody got along. But could we take on another?

"I want a dog that's like me," Tianna continued. "One that's differently abled."

"Me too," Gianna then chimed in. "For Christmas."

"I have to walk with a cane at school and everybody looks at me," Tianna said. "I want a dog who understands what it's like to be different."

Their request nearly blew me over. A "differently abled" dog? Where on earth would I find a pet like that? With Christmas only a few weeks away? Would a new dog even get along with the ones we already had?

"I'm not sure it makes sense," I said, trying to sound every bit the loving but reasonable adult. I didn't want to disappoint them. They had faced Herculean struggles

A "differently abled" dog? Where on earth would I find a pet like that? With Christmas only a few weeks away?

ever since their birth. We all had—the doctors' appointments, tests, therapy, cataract surgery. That they were doing as well as they were seemed miracle enough.

"It doesn't have to make sense," Tianna stated with the finality of a preteen who has made up her mind. I shook my head. Maybe God could make sense of this.

For the first few years of their lives, I'd get on the computer every night after they went to bed, searching for answers to the many problems they had, tracking down every possible solution or treatment, most of them dead ends. In the end I was left with more worries than anything else. I didn't want to be a mom like that, always worried. If I could only trust.

The day after the girls asked for a disabled dog, I had to take Skater to Sandy, the groomer. Sandy knows me well and takes good care of our pets. She loves dogs—in fact, her place is named Must Love Dogs—and if anybody could, she would understand my quandary.

"You'll never guess what the girls want for Christmas," I told her. "A differently abled dog. They want a pet that's like them."

"Sweet."

"But Sandy, we don't have room for any more dogs. We're not a kennel; we have a house with a living room, stairs, a backyard. You're different. You've got a business here. You can rescue dogs and find a place for them. I can't imagine what our four dogs would do if I brought in another one..." I looked around the store and my eye fell on a brown pit bull, even bigger than Chaos. "Like this one..."

"That's Carmella," Sandy said.

The dog's ears pricked up at the sound of her name. She turned her head and looked at Sandy, got up and limped across the room, her spine arched, her legs bowed. She could hardly walk.

"What happened to her?" I asked.

"Don't know for sure." Sandy bent down to scratch Carmella behind the ears. "I had to rescue her from a kill shelter. She'd been kept in a cage that was too small for too long. Didn't have any room to grow."

"How horrible," I said. I hated to think that someone would treat a dog like that, leaving her maimed. She wouldn't even be alive if it hadn't been for Sandy. Fat chance that anyone would want to adopt her. "She's lucky you found her," I said.

"Do you want her?" she asked.

"I told you, I don't see how we can take on another pet. What would the others do? What would Chaos do? It's too big a risk for me to trust it."

"Try it out and see. She *is* differently abled. Just what you said you wanted. You can bring her back if it doesn't work out."

I brought Chaos into Must Love Dogs the next day. I was expecting—or, rather, fearing—a face-off with growling and snarling or worse. *Lord,* I prayed, *let's not let this get out of hand.* The two animals walked around each other, sniffing. Then their tails started wagging. Soon they were playing. It was a scene out of the Peaceable Kingdom.

"A match made in heaven," Sandy said. "Carmella is my Christmas present to you."

A few days later, I brought Carmella home. "I have a surprise for you," I told the girls. Carmella waddled into their bedroom and jumped up onto the bottom bunk bed. It wasn't graceful in the least, her hind legs kicking at the air as she pulled herself forward. For a moment I thought she was going to fall right off. But her reward came with hugs from both sides. She was home.

I don't want to pretend that life with three Chihuahuas, one large pit bull, one differently abled pit bull and two differently abled daughters isn't hectic. There is always something, whether it's a challenge or a disappointment the girls faced at school or an emergency trip to the vet or a mess somebody made in the backyard. But we're happy. Very happy.

Not long ago, the girls and I were taking the dogs for a walk and someone stopped to ask about Carmella. I was about to explain what had happened to her and how we had found her. Instead it was Tianna who spoke up, not even hesitating to talk to a stranger. "We wanted a dog just like us," she said. "It made sense."

The girls aren't the only ones who have grown. The other day we were in the backyard, and Carmella hesitated at the bottom of the steps. Usually she went around to the front door, where there were no steps, but today she gazed at the stairs longingly. "Come on, Carmella, you can do it," the girls shouted. She looked around at us with her sweet eyes and then lunged forward. It was like her struggle to jump on that bunk bed the first day she joined us. One step at a time, she did it. When she reached the top, we all hooted and hollered. "You did it!"

She just had to trust. Like me. ✺

MUST LOVE DOGS
The twins' parents fell in love with Carmella too.

THE JOY OF *christmas wishes*

Our Quirky Family Tree

What was it about Christmas that I just couldn't resist?

by **KRISTY DEWBERRY,** Oklahoma City, Oklahoma

MY FRIENDS, according to their holiday Facebook posts, hosted perfect Christmases year after year. Families all smiles for the camera, posed so every face could be seen, children sitting still for the picture no matter how long it took, the entire clan wearing matching pajamas or Christmas sweaters. I had long ago resigned myself to the fact that that wasn't the Dewberry way. We were an authentic but loving mess of a family and didn't pretend otherwise. At times Christmas felt like a 20-car pileup, with heated disagreements and presents that would be returned. Last year, however, was messier than most, with unresolved hurts and broken relationships. All things considered, should I throw caution to the wind and try to bring everyone together no matter what? I didn't know where my relentless holiday spirit came from.

At a young age, I realized that my memories of Christmas past had a lot to do with what had gone wrong. There was the time Dad bought Mom a bread maker. I might have seen steam coming out of her ears when she unwrapped it. Did Dad think she needed to spend even more time in the kitchen? Apparently he had learned nothing from the previous Christmas. He'd given her a waffle iron, and her reaction told me she wanted to hit him over the head with it. Still, I loved Christmas.

The year I turned 12, Mom announced that I was too old for a stocking. I was outraged. I protested that my sister Kathy had gotten a stocking until she was 18. I liked the tradition. Mom had new rules, and that was that. Still, I loved Christmas.

My adult Christmases came with their own surprises. One Christmas my husband, Don, decided that our grandson Charlie would make a fine doctor and bought him an anatomy kit. "Why did you give me a skeleton for Christmas?" Charlie said, folding his arms in a pout. He was six. I'd warned Don at the store that our grandson was more likely to aspire to a career of serving slushies over doctoring at his age. Don and I got separate gifts. I won Charlie over with the plastic slushie machine. That year, I definitely loved Christmas.

Presents often seemed to stir up trouble in our family. It wasn't just the waffle iron and the anatomy kit. When my toddler granddaughter Joslyn got a play stroller for her dolls, she threw a fit. "I'm not a baby!" she screamed, thinking the stroller was meant for her. We had to move it to the garage to prevent any further meltdowns. Still, I loved Christmas.

I even loved Christmas when our poodle, Dinger, went missing for hours. The turkey dried out while we searched. I didn't love Christmas any less when Grandpa Pete had a heart attack, and we threw all the gifts in the trunk of the car and drove to Missouri in an ice storm. Even when Mom's assisted living center allowed no visitors due to Covid, I loved Christmas.

Last year, though, I really wanted our clan to come together even if circumstanc-

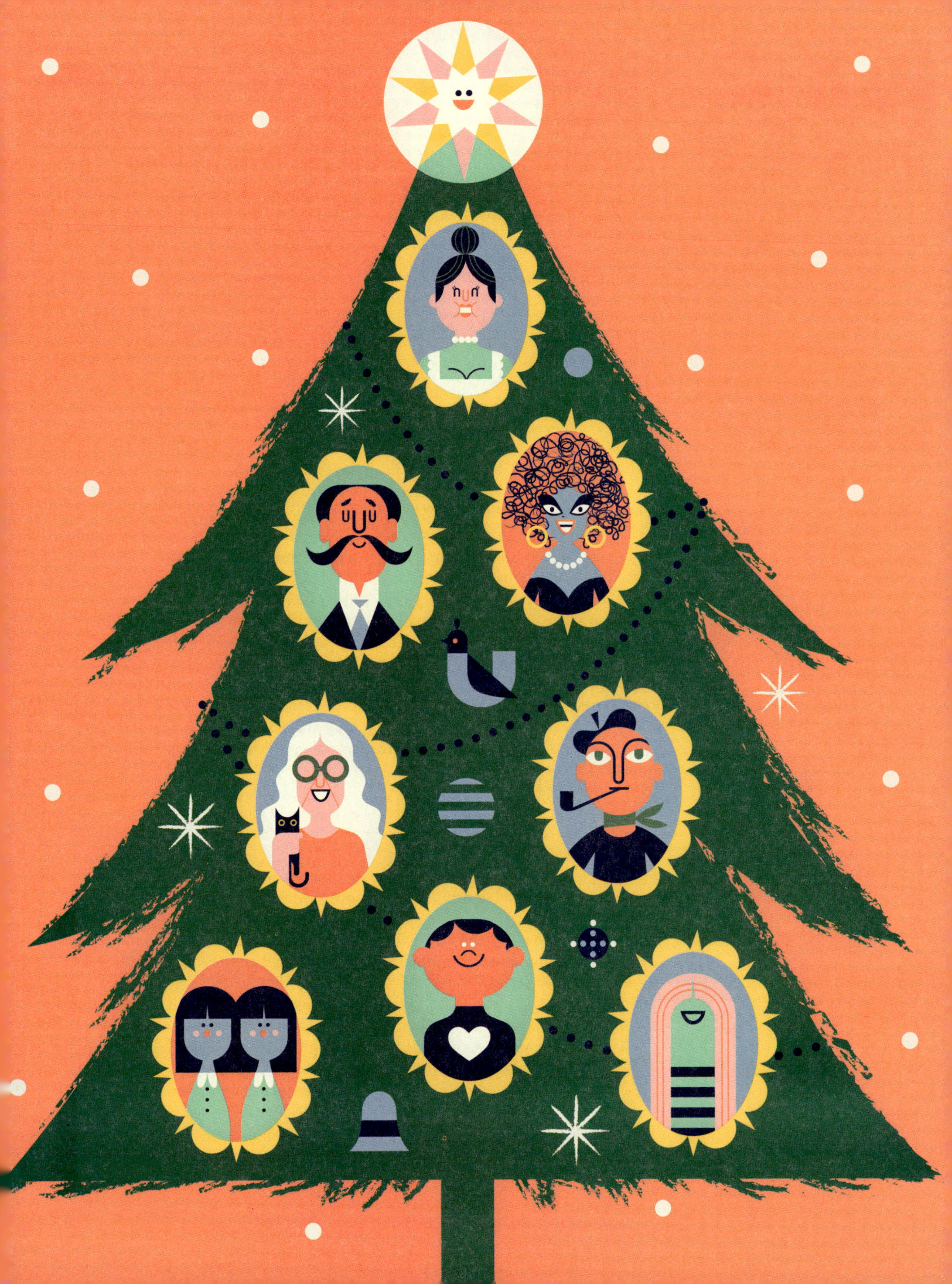

es seemed destined to test the limits of my holiday spirit. Family strife was at a high point. This one wasn't talking to that one. "What if we put on Christmas and nobody comes?" I asked Don one night. "There's a lot of conflict, and I probably don't know the half of it. I have to wonder if I'm a glutton for punishment."

Don shrugged. Some help. So I took Christmas to God. He wouldn't just shrug as Don had. I prayed about it and, sure enough, found inspiration. Why not have two Christmases, one early afternoon, one early evening? We'd celebrate in shifts. Everyone could pick a time slot that suited their schedule and, as a bonus, they could possibly steer clear of anyone they weren't getting along with at the moment. Genius! I spread the word. "Come at 1:00, or come at 5:30 when we serve the turkey. All are welcome anytime." Responses trickled in, some with caveats.

Our son, Brian, had recently remarried after a bitter divorce that his grown children, Charlie and Joslyn, were still angry about. Charlie had asked if his dad was coming. If so, Charlie was not ready to spend Christmas with him.

Our daughter Kelly's children, Haley and Tyler, had issues with their parents and each other. Haley had been accepted into an esteemed Oklahoma university, all expenses paid, but—without consulting her mother—had turned down the scholarship to stay in town with her boyfriend. When Haley asked if she could bring her boyfriend, I said "of course," without considering the consequences. As best I could, I tried to stay in my lane as a supportive grandmother and not get in the middle.

Haley's mother and stepdad weren't too happy with me for including the boyfriend who'd "ruined everything." Haley's big brother, Tyler, had strongly expressed his disappointment in his sister's choices, so there was a rift between the siblings. Family get-togethers meant everything to Tyler, and I knew he needed a break from his grueling schedule of working and volunteering to get himself through graduate school. I hoped he'd come.

Turned out, everyone except Brian showed up at 1:00. I set out finger foods, chips and dip, cookies, the works. Joslyn, who'd left strollers behind long ago, brought her famous deviled eggs. We played games and exchanged gifts. For once, everyone seemed pleased with their presents, and all the clothing fit just right. No waffle irons and no returns.

Most of the family stayed for the 5:30 Christmas, when Brian showed up. Charlie and Joslyn stayed long enough to greet him on his arrival. It was an encouraging first step. After all my worrying, the full house was an unexpected gift. We enjoyed the traditional turkey, which everyone agreed came out juicy and delicious. Perhaps satisfied tummies helped keep the mood light and forgiving. After dinner, we played bingo, always a crowd favorite. Haley and her boyfriend sat by me, and I got to know him. He was sweet, soft-spoken and polite, just the kind of young man a grandmother would approve of. I could tell Haley was glad I liked him.

I sat and watched my family, with all its tangles and quirks. I soaked up the laughter and conversation and ignored the few awkward interactions I stumbled upon. Christmas had come—and lasted for two shifts. No way could we organize ourselves for a photo for my Facebook friends to admire. But that hardly mattered.

Despite differences that come and go and conflicts that might divide us, we're a family held together by a love that runs deep. December 25 reminds me that Jesus was born for all of us, out of God's love for every one of us, just as we are, wonderfully imperfect. And that's why I will always love Christmas, dents and all! ✻

THE JOY OF *christmas wishes*

Warm Winter Wink

Perhaps she'd found a little blessing from above

by **LAURA KAYE**
New York, New York

IT WAS FREEZING by the time my shift ended at Broadway's Belasco Theatre, where I worked as an usher. I felt inside my pockets for my leather gloves. I was sure I had them on the way into work....

It wasn't easy earning a living in the Big Apple. God knew that even with this usher gig, I could barely cover my bills every month. I'd really wanted a pair of red gloves to match my purse, but I could only afford one pair and black was more practical. Now I didn't even have those.

Weeks later, rushing to make a weekday matinee, I almost stepped on a pair of red leather gloves lying on Eighth Avenue like a Christmas surprise. I picked them up and looked around to see who'd dropped them. People pushed past me, not paying me or the gloves any mind.

Except for two older women. "We saw you find them!" one of them said. "Aren't you lucky!"

"I should leave them somewhere," I said. "In case the owner comes back."

"By the time she realizes the gloves are gone, honey," the other lady assured me, "she won't even know where to look. Trust me, those gloves were meant for you. They even match your purse!"

The women waved to me as they wandered off. I stayed there in the street for several more minutes, just in case someone came to claim them. Finally I gave up and put them on. They fit...like a glove. ✷

CITY SIDEWALKS
Laura likes to people-watch at the fountain outside Lincoln Center.

THE JOY OF *christmas wishes*

Mom's Christmas Wish

Our search for a nostalgic Nativity seemed to be in vain

by **MARY WHITNEY,** Leavittsburg, Ohio

READER FAVORITE

MOM AND I LOOKED out at the pine trees lining the snow-covered yard of her new house. I was grateful to be able to spend time with her every day, now that my husband, John, and I had found her a place only five minutes from our own.

"What's your Christmas wish?" I asked.

Mom thought for a long moment. "I want a Nativity scene just like the one we had on our Christmas tree farm years ago," she said finally. "What's yours?"

At first I wasn't sure what to say. Mom had been diagnosed with breast cancer. There was a good chance this would be our last Christmas together. What did I want most of all? "To see you smile," I told her.

Mom touched my hand. "Sounds like we could both use that peaceful manger scene."

I grew up on a 62-acre tree farm. Families coming to get an evergreen for Christmas always stopped to admire the glowing plastic Nativity scene we set up in the snow. From sheep to wise men to the angel who watched over them all, every figure was colorfully painted.

"If that's what Mom wants for Christmas, I want to get it for her," I told John. How hard could it be to find a lighted outdoor Nativity?

Harder than we thought, it turned out. We drove around to all the stores we could think of, but the best we could do was Mary, Joseph and Jesus figurines from Kmart. "This really won't do," I said. "It's missing the shepherds and animals. There aren't even any wise men."

"Let's get the set for backup. Just in case we don't find anything else," John said. "Then we keep looking."

We tucked the Holy Family into the garage for safekeeping. I got in touch with relatives to see if, by some miracle, anyone still had that old set of Mom's. I searched eBay and Craigslist, but the few sets I found were too expensive once shipping costs were factored in.

Christmas was fast approaching. In between shopping, decorating the tree and planning holiday gatherings, John and I continued our search for the Nativity. Then Mom had to spend several days in the hospital. Visiting with her became our priority. Our Nativity search seemed to be over.

A few days before Christmas, with Mom back at home, John and I found a little time to relax. We built ourselves a crackling fire and sat down to watch a football game. When I glanced at John, he was looking off into the distance.

"What is it?" I said.

"I just remembered something I haven't thought of in decades," John said. "My parents had a Nativity scene when I was a little boy. The figures lit up when you plugged them in. Just like your mom's old set."

ILLUSTRATION BY GRIESBACH/MARTUCCI

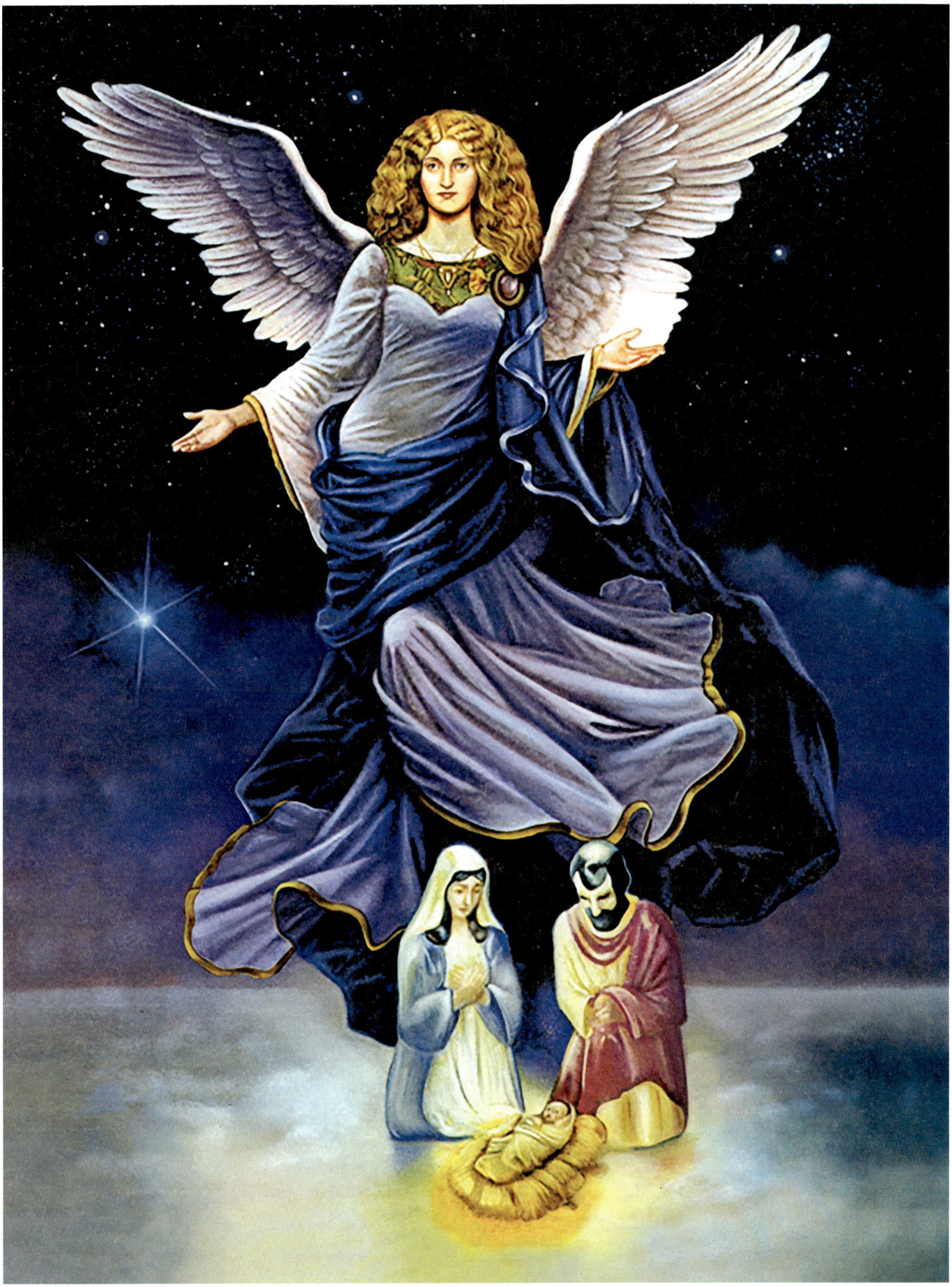

John's parents had died years before, but his family still owned the land they had lived on nearby. The only structure left on the property was a storage shed filled with who knew what. "Let's check out that shed first thing tomorrow!"

We drove over the next day and rummaged through the clutter. Lawn mowers, gardening tools, bicycles. I was about to give up hope when John suddenly cried out, "I see a shepherd!"

I pushed my way over to him. Sure enough, there was a tall shepherd holding a lamb. Next to him were three wise men, a camel and a cow. Even Mary. They were all looking pretty worse for wear, but there was no mistaking this was exactly the kind of scene Mom had in mind. "They're coming with us," I said.

Back home John went out on the frozen driveway and power-washed each figure. He even built a wooden manger for them. I bought metallic paint and set to work with my brushes to spruce them up. When the paint was dry I called John out to the garage.

"They look even better now than they did when I was a boy," he said. "I don't suppose they'd still light up after all this time."

I held my breath as we tested them. Each one worked perfectly. It was as if those years in the shed hadn't passed at all. For a moment I stood there admiring the figures—wise men, shepherds and animals, Mary. We'd add Joseph and Baby Jesus from the Kmart set.

And then I realized something terrible: The little scene was missing an angel.

"Two Marys and no angel," I said to John. But he had an idea. We set up the scene in Mom's yard as a surprise, arranging the figures in mounds of straw. Mary and Joseph huddled around their baby. The wise men brought their gifts. The shepherd clutched his lamb. For our duplicate Mary, we fashioned a pair of wings out of silver tinsel and turned her into a beautiful angel. Our search really was over.

When the sun went down, I led Mom to the window. John turned on the lights. Mom gasped. She was so surprised that at first she couldn't even speak. Then finally she said, "Thank you for making my Christmas wish come true." My Christmas wish came true too. ✷

FRONT-ROW SEAT
Mother (top left) and daughter share their glee over the main event in the backyard.

28 GUIDEPOSTS

THE JOY OF *christmas wishes*

Teamwork!

Would my husband ever just stop it with the holiday chores? He was doling them out like Christmas candy

by **ANNE MUNSON,** Tallahassee, Florida

One load of laundry was spinning in the dryer, and I was sorting the next load. I tended to the task slowly, very slowly. I hoped I'd found a quiet place to hide from my next assignment. It would come as a request, a friendly "Can you…?" from my husband.

When I took time off work for the holidays, I'd imagined relaxing over hot cocoa with our teenage daughters after a fun-filled day of baking cookies and wrapping presents. Maybe we'd spend afternoons on the sofa binge-watching Christmas movies. Seasonal bliss! But I was married to Noel, who—despite a name that literally meant Christmas—found a way to make our family togetherness all about getting things done. Couldn't we just chill?

I dropped a red turtleneck into the colors pile. *Noel never stops on an ordinary day,* I thought. *Why would he relax just because it's Christmastime?*

At that very moment, Noel passed the doorway with an armful of tiny lights for the front porch, which he decorated every year without fail. I hunched, quiet as a mouse, hoping he hadn't seen me. No such luck. Noel took a long stride backward and ducked his head into the laundry room. "Hey," he said, chipper as could be, "think you could change the litter box? It's pretty full." And off he went to make our house look festive.

That was Noel all over. He saw me in the middle of one thing and asked me if I'd mind doing something else. Probably because he was doing three things at once himself. In the early days of our marriage, I'd nicknamed him Multiple Priorities Man. Nothing was overlooked, and there was no time like the present to do all of it, especially once our family grew to the four of us. Somehow Noel had found four times as much stuff for us to do.

It was true I'd noticed earlier that the litter box needed attention, but I'd put it off. Which wasn't fair to the cat, I knew. I interrupted the laundry to take care of it before I forgot. My plan was to do it quickly and return to the laundry room, where I was relatively safe from our taskmaster.

In the kitchen, I found our daughters busy as bees. Heidi was at the sink doing the dishes. Her sister, Cate, was putting away the silverware. "The porch needs sweeping," Noel said when he ducked in to grab an extension cord from the pantry. "And the Christmas tree needs water."

"Sure thing, Dad."

"You girls are the best."

Cate and Heidi giggled and shrugged their shoulders. Heidi called "porch," while Cate said "tree." They didn't ever seem to be bothered by their father's never-ending to-do list.

"Your father runs a tight ship," I said.

the joys of Christmas

HANDS ON *Anne says the bandage on Noel's finger is the result of one of his holiday decorating projects.*

"Teamwork, teamwork," Cate said in a singsong voice.

"What's gonna work?" Heidi finished, laughing as she remembered a childhood song. Growing up, they'd heard Noel sing it a thousand times. Since Noel worked from home, he'd kept our household running smoothly for years. He got the girls to endless pediatrician appointments when they were little and picked them up from school when they were sick. If I had to work late, he helped with homework and cooked dinner. Happily. He took care of the yardwork, fixed our cars, even figured out how to resurrect a dying AC system by watching YouTube videos.

As soon as the girls were walking and talking, the tiny team members were carrying their weight. "Let's see you put all your toys away in their place," Noel had encouraged four-year-old Heidi. She proudly showed off her clean room when she was done. "Now that you are tall enough, you can empty the dishwasher," he'd told 10-year-old Cate, after showing her where everything went. Noel never forgot to thank them for their work. They embraced the responsibility that came with being on the family team.

As the only child of a single working mother, Noel had pitched in at home from an early age. Even while other kids were outside playing ball and running around the neighborhood. "I think my earliest memory is standing at the stove making ham and eggs," Noel had told me once with a laugh. "I needed a step stool to reach." He was so independent, I wondered if he'd even thought about asking for help.

I cleaned out the cat's box and poured in the fresh litter. Usually Noel's casual re-

30 GUIDEPOSTS

quests for me to do this or that weren't an issue. It was just his way. But today his "way" was just too much for me. Did everything have to be addressed right now? Or, some of it, ever at all? As far as I knew, *Better Homes and Gardens* wasn't coming by to do a holiday photo shoot.

I hadn't even sealed up the litter bag when Noel breezed by again. "I'm going to fill up the car," he said, jingling his keys like Santa's sleigh bells. "Could you—?"

"Um, no," I said, cutting him off. "Whatever it is, I can't. I'm going upstairs to take a shower."

The laundry was still waiting, but I needed a better hiding place. If I didn't get away from Noel now, I was afraid I might snap and say something I would regret. On my way upstairs, I heard Cate humming a Christmas carol while she dutifully watered the tree.

I shut the bathroom door behind me. *God, I can't ever get a moment's peace with this man! It's maddening! Please remind him it's Christmas break!* I guessed a break was wishful thinking in our house. Instead of enjoying my time off with my family, I was shut away in the bathroom. *Why can't we just be a family instead of a team?*

I turned on a hot shower and got in. *You need to cool down,* I told myself. I reached to adjust the temperature and felt a wave of guilt. Noel was a loving husband and father. It wasn't as if he was ordering us all around while he did nothing. He worked harder than anyone. He was always juggling projects so he could jump in to help us with anything we might need. Ready to run to the hardware store to make a repair, dig around in the attic for a forgotten box or whip up a meal. I had everything to be grateful for. Most days, Noel's inability to sit still—or let anyone else sit still either—was just another quirk I loved about him.

"Lord, I just don't have the energy to keep up. Please make him…" I stopped short. I'd just listed all that Noel did for our family. If I was going to pray for someone to change, it had to be me. "God, help me appreciate him, even when it's exhausting."

I stood under the showerhead, letting the water wash over me, waiting to feel the change take hold. I might be given more patience or perhaps a burst of enthusiasm. Instead, a single photo came to mind. One I'd seen of Noel as a child, with thick golden hair and a slight frame. A typical latchkey kid of the 1980s, the little man of the house, playing a big role. His family of two depended on it. I turned off the water and reached for a towel. *How wonderful it must be for Noel to finally have a whole team to rely on.* And how many times might he have wished as a young boy for just that?

Surely the girls and I were an answer to Noel's long-ago prayer. If I was part of his blessing from God, I wanted to live up to the role, to enjoy every minute of all that my family had been given by having one another. Especially at Christmas.

I went downstairs to finish the laundry and make myself available for whatever

> *Most days, Noel's inability to sit still—or let anyone else sit still either—was just another quirk I loved about him.*

new chore Noel was passing out to the team. In no time, he had one at the ready.

"Family project," Noel called. "Anne? Girls? It's time to get the Christmas village set up in the living room."

The girls came running, ready to arrange (and rearrange) all the houses and figurines they loved. I turned on the Christmas music, and Noel started some hot chocolate. I knew when the Christmas village was done, we would all settle on the couch to admire our hard work. What more could I wish for than spending the holidays with the best team ever assembled? ✳

THE JOY OF *christmas wishes*

Stamped With Love

My wife always handled the Christmas cards. Except one year

by **RICHARD H. SCHNEIDER,** Roving Editor

READER FAVORITE

MY WIFE, BETTY, handled the big job of sending out our family Christmas cards every year. All I did was seal and stamp the envelopes, and that was just fine with me. Writing the cards always seemed like an ordeal. We'd set up at the dining table with the huge pile of cards, and Betty would spend the evening with her head down, writing away. But then came the year when the whole job landed on my shoulders.

Betty had gone into the hospital in early November with a back problem, and her doctors thought she might have to stay there through Christmas. Thanksgiving came and went, and I avoided the boxes of cards we had picked out, praying she'd be home in time to do them. However, by mid-December, I reluctantly decided that if any of our friends were going to hear from us that year, I'd better get cracking. I stacked the boxes of cards and rolls of stamps on the dining room table, along with Betty's seemingly endless list of names and addresses. I steeled myself to my task, deciding to do 10 cards each night. That would probably get most of them out in time for the holiday.

Our two boys had already gone to bed, and the house was silent. I needed to get in the mood, so I put on a CD of Christmas classics. Soon the croons of Bing Crosby filled the air. Pen in hand, I started to write. I signed the cards "Merry Christmas from Betty, Dick and the boys." With the seventh card I began to appreciate what Betty had gone through in years past. After the tenth, I was ready for bed.

The next day, I forced myself to keep slogging through the imposing pile. And so it went until I picked up the card to go to Gordon and Joan Lockyer. Their names struck a real chord. I remembered when the four of us first became friends. Gordon invited us up to Lake Geneva, Wisconsin, where he kept a small sailboat, and Betty and I spent a beautiful day on the sun-sparkled waters. Until then I had done very little sailing, but that day awakened a passion. I later owned several sailboats and enjoyed many happy years cruising waters from Lake Michigan to Long Island Sound. I realized I had a personal note for Gordon and Joan, and I wrote a few words about that long-ago day on Lake Geneva.

By the time I finished my note, I thought how nice it would be if I could share similar memories with our other friends. The next card was for Dick and Jill Lillard. We had never sailed together, but we'd spent many

New Year's Eves at the wonderful parties they threw. My spirits lifted even more when I saw the next name on the list—my boyhood friend Harry Sandberg. I had fun reminding him about the times we used to play with our electric trains.

And then there was the couple on whose card I wrote, "I'm thinking of how much Betty and I enjoyed your son's wedding last year."

I found myself looking forward to spending time with good friends. No longer did the cards feel like a chore. Each one was a mini reunion. When I saw the name of an old friend from my childhood church, the words flowed: "Remember that Christmas when our pastor read *A Christmas Carol* to our youth group while we were gathered around his fireplace?"

Before I knew it, all of our cards were written, signed and sealed, stamped and mailed. All in time to reach our friends and family before Christmas.

A few days later, I got the call that Betty was being released from the hospital early. As we drove home, she said, "I'm so sorry that I let you down by not doing the cards this year."

"On the contrary," I said. "I've never been more in the Christmas spirit!" ✶

MYSTERIOUS WAYS

No Traffic

THERE'S ONE GOOD *thing about being on the road Christmas Day*, I thought, driving from my parents' house in Richmond, Virginia, back to Charlotte, North Carolina. *No traffic.* I'd barely seen another car on the interstate all day. Most people were home with their families. But not me. I was a policewoman, new enough on the force that I didn't get a choice of shifts. I'd managed to score time off Christmas Eve, but I had to be back on duty tonight. My sergeant made it clear: "Be here for roll call before the midnight shift." It was a four-hour drive to my parents' house; I'd only had time to eat dinner and exchange gifts before I hit the road again.

Near the Carolina state line, my car started to cough. First a hiccup, then a full-blown hack. I pulled off at the next exit. Two-thirds of the way up the ramp, the engine died. *What do I do now?* I got out and looked around. There was a service station down the road, closed for the holiday. I could call a tow truck, but who was available on Christmas Day? What if I didn't make it in time for my shift? My sergeant would never believe that I hadn't been waylaid by eggnog and Christmas cookies.

Just then a lone car approached on the interstate. A blue El Camino. *Haven't seen one of those in years.* The driver slowed and pulled off next to me. He rolled down his window. "I'm the mechanic. What seems to be the problem?"

I couldn't believe my luck! I explained how the car died. In less than three minutes, the man popped the distributor cap, opened the points, cleaned the contacts and told me to try starting the engine. My car roared to life. "Thank you!" I said, offering him the money in my wallet.

The man shook his head. "No charge on Christmas. Good thing I was in my shop when you called."

My eyes went wide. "I didn't call. I'd just broken down when you pulled up."

"I guess the driver who called is farther down the interstate. Better find her." He got in his car and drove off. I got on the road too.

Only when I was back in Charlotte—well before roll call—did it occur to me: I'd passed plenty of mile markers and exits farther down the interstate, but I never did see the disabled car that had summoned the mechanic.

—AMY BRADY, CHARLOTTE, NORTH CAROLINA

THE JOY OF
God's Grace

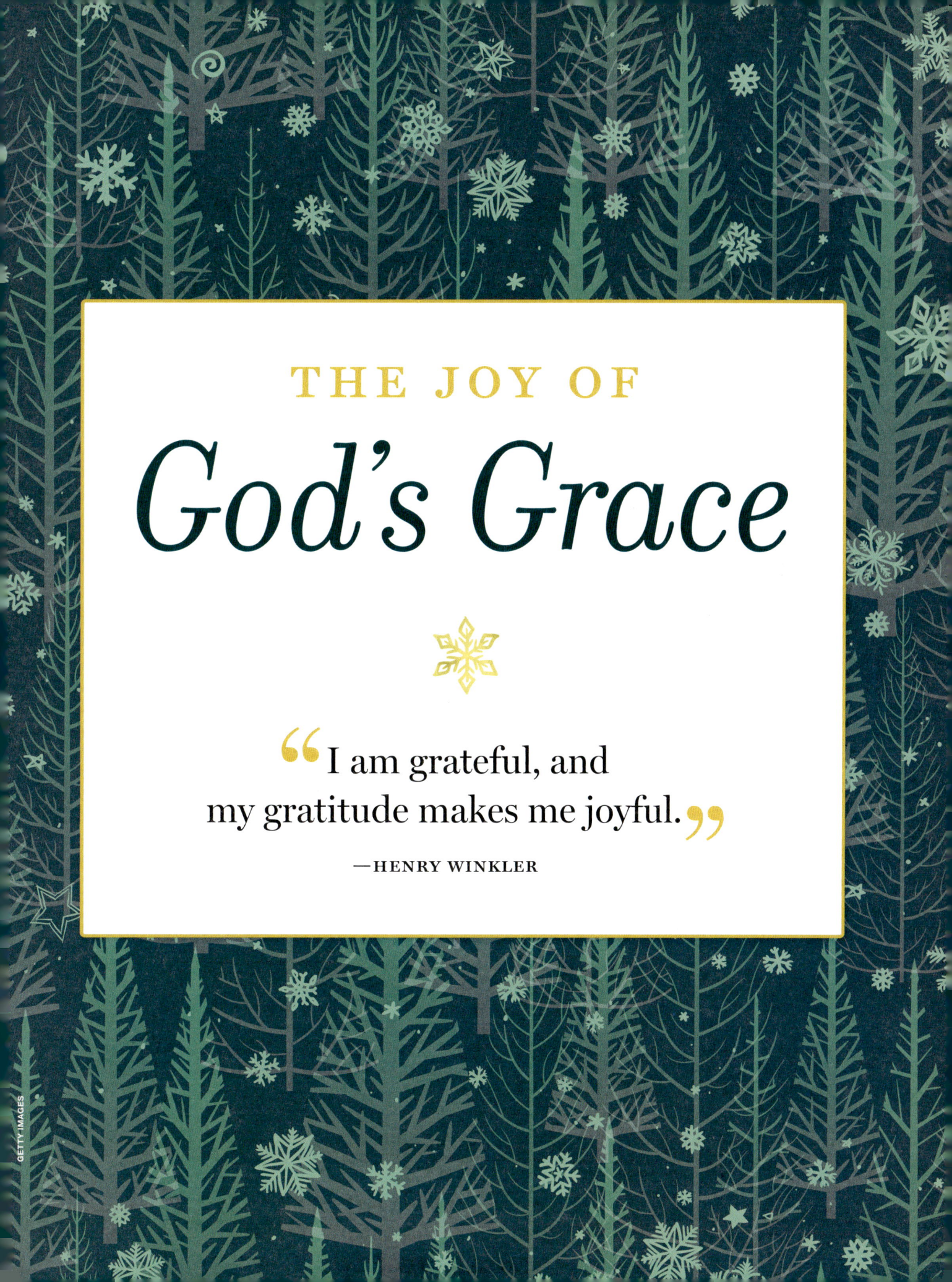

"I am grateful, and my gratitude makes me joyful."

—HENRY WINKLER

THE JOY OF *god's grace*

Comfort and Joy

Everybody knows how much Linus loves his blue blanket. There was a special blanket in my life too

by **DIANE STARK,** Brazil, Indiana

I FOUND A SEAT by myself near the back of the auditorium for the high school production of *A Charlie Brown Christmas.* My son Nathan was singing in the choir, and I'd ducked into the morning performance before I got lost in the running around that would make up my day.

The rest of my family had tickets for that evening, but I had a church youth group commitment at the same time. No one was surprised. All I did, it felt like, was run from one obligation to the next, too busy to stop and feel anything in the way of holiday spirit—unless exhaustion counted. Even if I was just going through the motions in an overscheduled daze, it was better than the alternative. If I kept moving, I wouldn't have a free moment to dwell on what had happened three years before. The lights went down, and I listened for my son's voice in the opening song, "Christmas Time Is Here." I wished it wasn't.

My stepdad, Doug, who'd been a father to me in every way that mattered, had suffered a fatal heart attack on Christmas Day 2021. The loss had turned the most wonderful time of the year into the most painful time of my life. And now, in what had become my December habit, I got involved in any holiday activity that would have me. If I stopped to catch my breath, I feared that grief would overwhelm me. My stepdad was gone, and with him went the comfort I'd always known this time of year.

The curtain went up, and I stifled a yawn thinking of the day ahead. I had agreed to squeeze in an early lunch with a friend I'd already canceled on once because of a scheduling conflict. After lunch, I'd pick up the supplies for movie night with our church youth group. That meant two stops—one at the grocery for a carload of drinks and snacks, and one at the party store for paper products. I'd insisted I didn't need any help setting everything up before the event. I told the other parent volunteers that I'd also show up early enough to arrange the folding chairs myself. "I need the exercise," I'd said.

My yawn made it obvious to me that

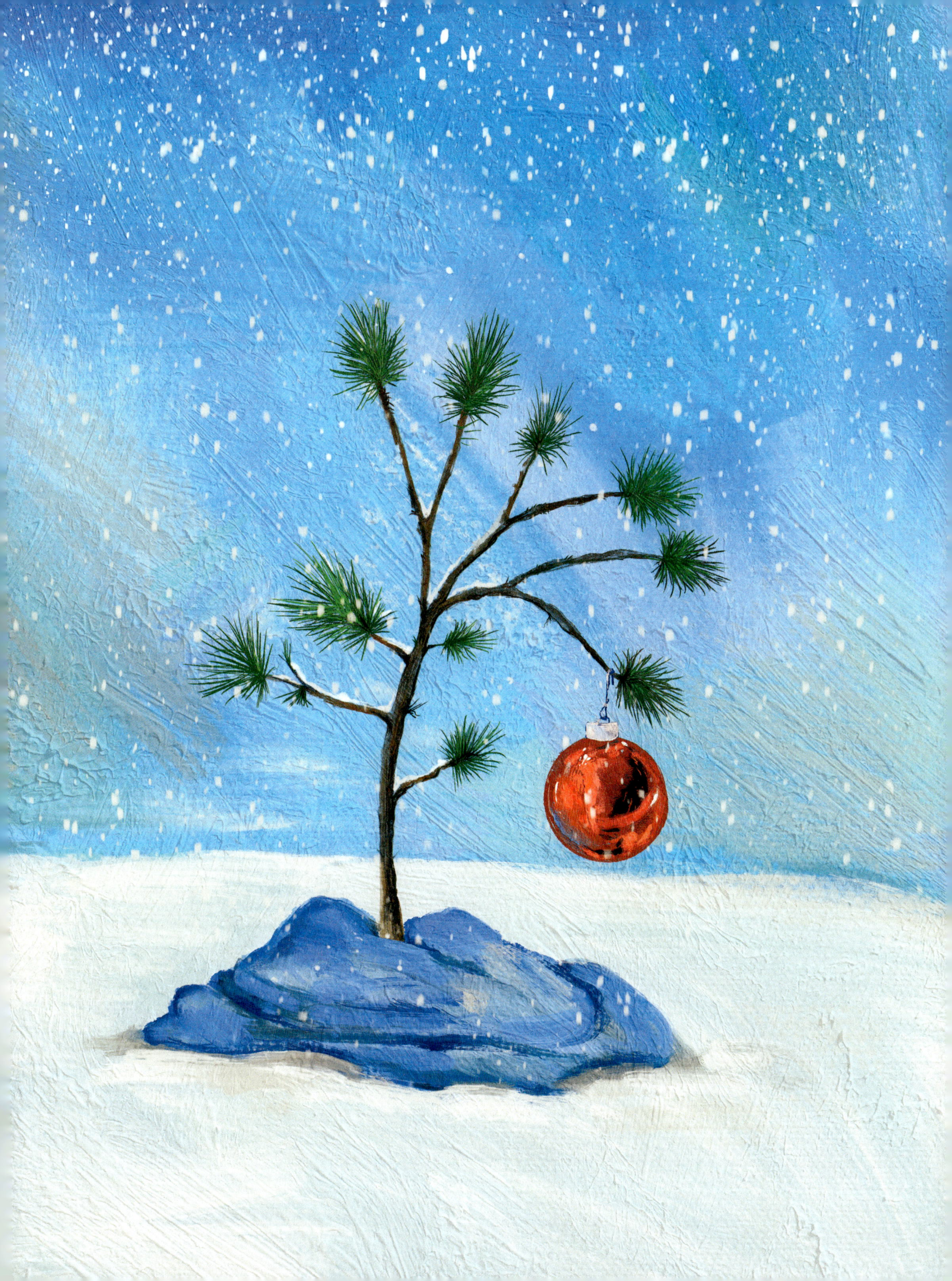

what my body really needed was to slow down. But I was afraid to. As much as I loved hearing my son sing, I felt too vulnerable to sit still and be fully in the moment. I needed distractions to get me through the season.

The spotlight hit the tall student playing Charlie Brown in that familiar yellow shirt with a black zigzag on the chest. He walked across the stage with his buddy Linus, who was dragging his signature blanket. I half-listened while Charlie Brown confessed that the season left him feeling down. I knew the storyline and the happy ending. I was here for Nathan's singing.

On stage, Charlie Brown leaned against a red doghouse decorated with Christmas lights. He reached over to pet the stuffed white Snoopy perched on the roof. That reminded me: I should grab a bag of dog food since I was going to the grocery store anyway. In fact, I'd grab a few other things we were running low on. I ran through a checklist in my head.

"Charlie Brown, you need involvement!" a female student said with such conviction

> *My stepdad was gone, and with him went the comfort I'd always known this time of year.*

that I was pulled back into the play. Charlie Brown was sitting on a stool at the window of a wooden storefront. "Psychiatric Help—Five Cents," the sign said. Lucy held forth on the other side of the window, having her say about how Charlie Brown could feel better. "You need to get involved in some real Christmas project."

How is that working out for me? I wondered. Could I ever take on enough projects to feel good about Christmas again? I doubted Lucy's advice was worth the nickel she was charging for it. A few scenes later, I watched Charlie Brown hang a single ornament on his sad little tree. The sapling couldn't handle the weight and bent all the way to the ground. *If I add one more thing to my schedule, I'm going to collapse too.*

It had been weeks since I'd taken a minute for myself. But that was the point, wasn't it? I didn't want to sit in the quiet. I didn't want to think. Didn't want to feel. I barely made time for prayer because I didn't know what to pray for. Comfort was beyond my reach. And joy? It wasn't fair for me to ask God for something there was no way he could give me. "Stay busy," I kept telling myself. "Push through December, and you'll feel better after it's over." I might not have agreed with Lucy's advice, but I wasn't so sure my strategy was working either.

With Charlie Brown offstage, Linus gently straightened the drooping sapling. The other kids pitched in to decorate it as a surprise for their friend. Linus unfurled his reliable old blanket and wrapped it around the base of the tree. The tree held its own, secure and loved. The blanket had made all the difference. "Merry Christmas, Charlie Brown," his friends cheered, and all was well. The choir joined the cast onstage to sing the closing songs.

As the actors took their bows, I noticed the boy who played Linus pick up the blanket and toss it over his shoulder. I wondered if the blanket had come from his own bed at home, because it seemed like much more to him than a prop in a play. He ran his fingers over the silky edge, as if he were familiar with its soft comfort.

There had been a blanket like that in my own life. The throw Doug had bought as a souvenir on a long-ago family vacation in Gatlinburg, Tennessee. The blanket featured a Great Smoky Mountains landscape, where we'd done a fair share of hiking. I could picture Doug spreading the blanket out on the couch and patting the space beside him, inviting his dogs or grandkids to snuggle up next to him. I couldn't count how many times I'd witnessed the cozy scene. In my mind's eye, I watched one picture fade into another, smiling to myself at those memories.

Nathan probably didn't see me wave to him as the choir left the stage. Linus walked off with his blanket. *Maybe I want to wrap myself in the cozy comfort of my memories for a while.* On the spot, I decided to change my afternoon plans.

I texted my friend to postpone our lunch one more time. "I'll fill you in when we see each other," I told her. I called on a couple other parent volunteers to pick up the supplies for movie night. "I'll be there to help set up, but I need to spend some time recharging," I said.

Driving home, I realized I wasn't sure what had happened to that Great Smoky Mountains blanket. I didn't have it. Instead I'd kept a few of Doug's favorite T-shirts that were too hard to part with.

At home I dug one out of my closet and slipped the way-too-big tee over my head. In the quiet, I settled on the couch with a favorite photo album of Doug and my kids when they were little. In some, I could just make out the corner of that souvenir blanket. The tears came, but this time, I didn't try to hide from them. "God, thank you for bringing Doug into my life," I said. "Help me deal with my grief, so I can love Christmas again."

Every day I carved out time to sit with God and talk to him about Doug and how much I missed him. It wasn't easy, but it was a relief to let it all out, even if I fell apart sometimes. My family understood when I sneaked off alone for a while to cry or just to remember. In the end, I felt all the more joyful, knowing that Doug's loving spirit was still very much with me in our festivities at home and in fulfilling my (pared down) seasonal commitments.

Comfort may have seemed beyond my reach, but God's arms were long. He was there waiting to hold me as soon as I was ready to sit still in his embrace. Like the little sapling held safe in Linus's blanket, I was wrapped in the love that was the reason for the season. With the Peanuts crew, I could again say with gusto, "Merry Christmas, Charlie Brown!" ✷

WARM MEMORIES *Diane, here with her family (starring Nathan, second from right), rediscovered her love of Christmas.*

the joys of Christmas 39

THE JOY OF *god's grace*

Best Gift *Ever*

Tea drinkers can be very particular about their mugs. Ask these two

by **MEG BELVISO,** New York, New York

Better to give than receive, they say. I felt the truth of the proverb as I wrapped my roommate Kirsten's Christmas present last year. We'd agreed to exchange gifts when I returned to the apartment after spending the holiday with my family. There would be no quick, "Wow, thank you!" for this surprise. I wanted to be around to hear Kirsten delighting over what I'd gotten her every time she used it. "Best gift ever," I told her Pomeranian, Juniper, as he watched me put a bow on it.

Kirsten and I are both big tea drinkers. She sipped tea all day long, always from her bright yellow mug decorated with bees. "It's the perfect size," she often said, "and the color really makes me cheerful!" She especially liked the single bee stamped on the inside near the rim. "The perfect water line!" she claimed. In chilly weather, the cup also proved the perfect shape for her to wrap her hands around for warmth. To Kirsten, the mug was perfect, period. Until disaster struck. From my room one fall day, I heard a crash. I ran to the kitchen to find the floor covered in bright yellow ceramic shards and my roommate on her knees with the dustpan. "I slipped in my socks," she groaned, shooing Juniper away so she could sweep up. She went back to the store where she'd bought the bee mug but came home disappointed. "Everything's already got a Christmas theme," she said. "This was the best I could do." An off-white mug, similar in size, decorated with paw prints. "I really miss the bees."

The perfect mug seemed to be lost forever, but just in case, I secretly searched the internet. Over several days, I found a single bee on a white mug, a tall mug painted like a honeycomb, a mug that read "Let it..." with a bee at the end. There were plenty of bee mugs out there, just not Kirsten's. And then, unbelievably, in mid-December, one popped up on eBay. I jumped on it. Now it was wrapped and waiting with a bow on top. "The bees are back!" I told Juniper, whom I trusted to keep this quiet.

I tucked the gift away in my closet and packed for my holiday train ride. Before leaving the next day, I wouldn't even say the word *mug* out loud for fear of dropping a hint. If Kirsten unwrapped the surprise in time for her first morning cup after I got back, I'd have the whole day to feel like a Christmas hero with each new tea bag she dropped in to steep.

In the morning, I eyed the carefully hidden gift and threw an extra sweater into my travel bag. Time to catch my train. I rolled my luggage out of my room, grabbed my coat and was about to call, "Goodbye," when I heard it—another terrible crash in the kitchen. I ran in to find Juniper being shooed off once again, the paw mug in pieces on the floor. "I was just starting to get used to it," Kirsten said with a sigh.

Oh no! God, why put me in this posi-

tion? If I let her open the mug now, I'd barely have time to savor the moment before I had to rush out the door. *Hold off until you get back as planned*, I thought. *She can survive a few sad days with one of the backup mugs.*

Juniper licked my ankle as if questioning my next step. Did I really want my friend to spend even one sad day, at Christmas, no less? The excitement building in me seemed to be less about giving than it was about receiving praise for what I was giving. I was better than that, and perhaps I'd been put in just the right position to save me from myself.

I retrieved Kirsten's present from my closet and set it on the kitchen counter. "Merry Christmas!" Juniper watched from the swept floor.

Kirsten unwrapped the box and looked up at me while she opened it. "This is nice of you," she said, "but I'm not sure anything could cheer me up right now."

She lifted the tissue paper and gasped. She knew what it was as soon as she saw the lone yellow bee flying at the water line. It never occurred to her that the box may have held the *only* thing that could have cheered her up. Like a surprise on steroids.

The bees came back just when she needed them, just as my better self came back to me. I was sure Juniper smiled at me before I rushed off to catch my train. Maybe God did too. ✶

STOOP SIT *Meg, Kirsten and Juniper say, "Cheers!"*

the joys of Christmas 41

THE JOY OF *god's grace*

Destination Christmas!

Penguins, hippos, sharks and sea turtles made our December 25 a day to remember

by **GLORIA JOYCE,** Willow Grove, Pennsylvania

"What are we going to do on Christmas?" my 18-year-old daughter, Cassidy, home from college, asked one December night as we were loading the dishwasher. I'd been asking myself the same question and hadn't found an answer. Now we were down to the wire, and I needed to come up with a plan.

"Aunt Linda's still pretty mad, huh?" Cassidy said as I handed her a plate.

Normally we spent the day with family—my sister, Linda, and our parents. Linda was hosting this year, and that was the problem. I'd gotten us disinvited.

"None of this is your fault, Cassidy," I said, not for the first time.

In fact, the whole situation was just one big misunderstanding. I could have kicked myself for letting it go this far. It all started while I was having lunch with Linda in the spring. She asked about Cassidy's high school graduation ceremony date. "I want to get it on my calendar," she said. "It's my goddaughter we're talking about!"

Cassidy and her 15-year-old sister, Ana, were homeschooled. The program the girls followed offered a regional in-person graduation event in June. I let Cassidy choose that option, and she was over the moon about celebrating with so many kids in her peer group. I explained to Linda that we'd be traveling from Pennsylvania to Virginia for the big day. Even before I finished telling her how excited Cassidy was, I could feel the chill.

"We'd have loved for you to come," I said. "But tickets were limited to immediate family. You can watch it on a livestream..." Too late. My sister's nose was already out of joint. Even if we had a ticket for her, she wasn't up for traveling. She said I should have gotten her input first. Maybe I should have discussed it with her, or at least prepared her for the possibility, before we'd committed. Linda felt slighted, but I wouldn't have disappointed my daughter for anything. In fact, the huge graduation turned out to be a wonderful experience for Cassidy, a little bit of an introduction to what "regular school" would be like at an in-person college full of young people. She'd made the fall transition just fine.

I tried to reach out to Linda a few times, but it was no use. Linda could be a world-class grudge holder. She just needed to work through her feelings, and I knew she would. She'd return to being a loving aunt and godmother eventually but not in time for Christmas. Not this year.

Which left me to come up with something fun and memorable to do on Christmas Day, something to distract the girls from the fact that we weren't having our usual family get-together. Sure, we'd still see their grandparents on Christmas Eve, and there was nothing wrong with spending a quiet little Christmas at home. Still, I felt it was on me to make this Christmas special given the circumstances.

Cassidy and I finished the dishes. "I'm thinking about our Christmas, don't worry," I said. Cassidy kissed me on the cheek and went on her way. *Now what, Lord? I'm thinking all right, but I have zero ideas.*

I wondered if I might have found one while I sorted through the mail the next day. I opened a surprise Christmas card from my fun-loving aunt Helen in Florida. She'd included a check and a note saying, "Don't you dare use this for anything practical. Take the girls for a real adventure!"

Adventure. Could the word have been some kind of a God nudge? Last summer

DEEP DIVE *Joyce and her family wait for Scuba Santa to make an appearance at the aquarium's underwater tree.*

the joys of Christmas 43

we'd planned a visit to Adventure Aquarium, about 45 minutes away in Camden, New Jersey. We had to cancel when Ana caught a bad cold. We'd never rescheduled.

My husband, Matt, joined me at the kitchen counter. I showed him Aunt Helen's card. "What do you think about finally having a fun day at the aquarium?"

"Tickets are probably limited around the holiday weekend," he said, "but I bet we could get in before Cassidy goes back to college. Great idea."

I went to the aquarium's website to see what was available. The banner on the home page said, "Open Christmas!" Really? I clicked on *December 25* and hit *4*. When the cost of the tickets exactly equaled Aunt Helen's check, I was sure the aquarium was more than a God nudge. It was a full-on answer to prayer. I completed my purchase and raised my hands in the air. "We're spending Christmas Day at Adventure Aquarium!" I announced.

After church on Christmas morning, we changed into our favorite holiday sweatshirts, put our coats back on and went off on our adventure. I was overjoyed that the aquarium was open for our family, but I couldn't help thinking about the employees who were giving up time with theirs. So, when Matt pulled into a Wawa convenience store to gas up in his Santa hat, I dashed inside and bought six gift cards redeemable for sandwiches. It would be fun to treat some of the workers to lunch. Back in the car, the girls gave me puzzled looks. "We're going to hand them out to show our appreciation to the employees who came in for people like us today."

We spent the drive singing carols and writing thank-yous on the gift card envelopes. "Thank you for making our Christmas special!" "Lunch is on us!" "Happy holidays!" By the time we reached our destination, we were as excited about the gift cards as we were about the exhibits.

Our first "victim" was the girl who checked our tickets. When she handed them back, Ana left a card on the counter. "Hey, you forgot something," the girl called as we walked away.

"That's for you!" Cassidy said. "Merry Christmas!"

First stop, Penguin Park, where we were charmed by a waddle of African penguins who were getting extra sardines for Christmas. Ana slipped a gift card to a security guard. He looked surprised, then tipped his hat. At the stingray exhibit Cassidy handed a card to the young woman finishing up her presentation. "Wow," she said. "Thanks!"

On we went, spreading cheer from Pirate's Passage to Sea Turtle Cove to the Stingray Beach Club. As I watched the girls—and Matt too—ooh and aah at Kaleidoscope Cove, I couldn't help but wonder at God's goodness and how he turned this Christmas into something memorable in the best way. I pulled out my phone to document it. "Selfie!" I said. Matt and the girls turned around, and I snapped our picture to share with Aunt Helen down in Florida. It was time to head home.

"We have to pick up the souvenir photo taken when we first walked in," Cassidy said. As the clerk rang up the sale, I reached into my purse for the last of the gift cards.

"I get one too?" the clerk said. It seemed we had been making news among the workers. "You folks are like Santa Claus!"

We rode home in comfortable silence. I pulled out the souvenir photo and stared at my family, frozen in time. The girls with their smiles, playacting to be the center of attention. Matt with his whimsical two-tailed Santa hat, because one pom-pom just wasn't enough. And me, holding the gift envelopes and looking for all the world like this was exactly the Christmas I'd always dreamed of. In a sense it was. Because it was a Christmas only God himself could have arranged. ✴

THE JOY OF *god's grace*

Smudges on the Window

The house wasn't empty. Not completely

by **DIANE KALUSNIAK,** Grand Haven, Michigan

THE SILENCE inside my small house made it feel huge and empty. No laughter. No little feet padding around. No clinking silverware, crinkling gift wrap or squeals of surprise. I peered through the streaky glass of the sliding doors to my backyard, a window to a typical winter day in Michigan—gray and dreary. That's how I felt too. The holidays were over, and I was alone again.

On Christmas Eve, my house had overflowed with family—my three children, their spouses and my nine grandchildren. We spent the afternoon devouring appetizers and decorating cookies. My grandkids enjoyed the unseasonably warm weather, racing in and out to the backyard to play. We ate a big, hearty dinner—a baked ham, cheesy potatoes, green bean casserole and, for dessert, my specialty, cheesecake. Then we gathered around the tree in the living room to exchange gifts. I tried to keep it all organized, but the excitement quickly descended into paper-shredding chaos. Finally, we attended church with some very sleepy children.

The next afternoon, everyone went home. It felt unfair. Why couldn't Christmas last?

A little housekeeping would distract me, I decided. *Got to keep busy.* First, those streaky sliding glass doors. I grabbed a bottle of Windex and was poised to spray when the sun burst through the clouds. Light filled my backyard and streamed through the glass.

What I saw was my family, from the bottom, the tiny handprint of my 13-month-old grandson, to the top, the hand of his oldest cousin, who'd helped him slide the door. In between, the prints of all my kids and grandkids overlapped, tender mementos of our Christmas Eve joy.

I put down the Windex. The glass could wait. I'd hold on to my reminder of the love that surrounds me all throughout the year, a love that fills the silence. ✹

THE JOY OF *god's grace*

Sadie, You Are Loved

An English sheepdog and standard poodle mix, our sheepadoodle puppy was all legs and feet and not sure she could trust me

by **LYNNE HARTKE,** Chandler, Arizona

Our neighbors were hanging Christmas lights as I walked by with our dog, Sadie. I hadn't even thought about putting up house decorations. For weeks, I'd devoted all my time to teaching our big puppy to pee outside. Sadie and I walked up and down the block and around the neighborhood park. "Go potty," I urged when she sniffed the base of a light pole. A garbage can. A bench. Finally, she squatted! I might have seen two drops. "Good girl!" It was something. But not enough. I expected her to have mastered this by now.

After we'd lost our terrier late last summer, my husband, Kevin, and I planned to wait until the new year before getting another dog. We were part of the leadership team at church, and with our day jobs, our schedules were crazy around the holiday season. It was no time to be putting life on hold while we dealt with a puppy. Our plan went out the window when an acquaintance needed to rehome an eight-month-old sheepadoodle right away. An English sheepdog and standard poodle mix, Sadie was all legs and feet. Her head came up to my waist. She was 60 pounds, full of energy and untrained. Completely untrained. And as lovable as a giant stuffed animal. It wasn't even Thanksgiving yet, but I couldn't say no. Even though most of the responsibility would fall to me, since I worked from home.

In six weeks, we'd made a lot of headway with breaking some of those puppy habits. Sadie no longer jumped up to greet us or rested her head on the dinner table or sniffed the prickly pear cactus on our walks. Leash training discouraged her from rushing to say hello to other dogs or lunging to attack every leaf that blew across the sidewalk. But I seemed to be getting nowhere with her bladder control.

Most of Sadie's accidents happened when she was anxious, especially when she thought I was leaving her. Within days of her arrival, I had become "her person." She followed me everywhere. To the laundry room. Around the kitchen. To my desk. I was available to take her into the backyard many times a day. We went on morning and evening walks.

If I left the house, it was never for long. In fact, it didn't matter if I disappeared into another room or ran out to do a quick errand, the result was the same. Sadie peed on the carpet. On the tile floor. In her kennel. Near her kennel. On the couch. On a pile of clean blankets. The two drops she deposited at the park were a small victory.

I came in from our walk to find Kevin at his computer. "Good news," I said. "Sadie peed outside. Well, a little."

"Excellent. She'll get the hang of it eventually." Kevin threw a toy, and Sadie fetched it. She enjoyed Kevin's company, but he could come and go without incident. I worried I'd never be able to have that luxury.

"The neighbors are putting their lights up right on schedule," I said. "No puppy training to distract them, I guess."

"I'll bring the decorations down from the attic," Kevin said. "What about a tree?"

"We'll get a small one for that table in the corner."

"Really? Not a big standing one as usual? We have so many ornaments...."

I pointed at Sadie.

Kevin laughed. "Oh, yes, our klutzy puppy who hasn't grown into her feet." On the rare occasions Sadie lost sight of me, she zipped through the house at high speed, slipping and sliding on the tile, her legs flailing in all directions. A tree wouldn't stand a chance.

"Speaking of Christmas," Kevin said, "do you know what you'll talk about at the Christmas Eve service?"

I had been asked to share a message as I had in years past, and it wasn't easy to come up with a fresh idea. "I'm devoting all my creative energy to solving the peeing problem, so no, I haven't put my mind to the talk."

"Maybe Sadie will inspire you," Kevin said.

"Unlikely. I'm off to meet a friend for some advice, though. She has two rehomed dogs herself. Will you let Sadie out in a little while, please?"

PUPPY LOVE *Lynne and her energetic sheepadoodle, Sadie*

the joys of Christmas 47

I grabbed my car keys. They jingled in my hand. Sadie looked at them. At the door. At me. She promptly squatted on the carpet and released an ocean. "Oh, Sadie, please, nooo..."

"Go to your appointment," Kevin said. "I'll take care of it."

While I gave my friend an earful, I realized how hopeless and frustrated I sounded. "I'm trying to be patient, but at this point I'm wondering if I'll ever have a good and trained companion."

"Does Sadie snarl or bite?" my friend asked.

"Oh, no. She's not a biter or a digger. Isn't interested in the garbage. She rarely barks and doesn't destroy things. Not even her soft toys. She loves to play with her tennis ball."

"Sounds like she's a gentle girl but an active puppy," my friend said. "A puppy who doesn't want to lose another human."

"Doesn't she know better by now?"

"It will take time for her to get comfortable with the idea. To trust you. I watched it

> *I'd do whatever I could to help Sadie become the best companion she could be. She deserved that.*

happen with my own dogs, each learning in their own time. Be consistent, give Sadie some grace, and all of a sudden, she'll get the message."

I returned home somewhat encouraged. "Let's put up those lights," I said to Kevin.

Sadie supervised from the front window while we strung the strands. I think she smiled a little when she saw them twinkling along the eaves after our evening walk. How could I ever lose patience with her? I'd do whatever I could to help Sadie become the best companion she could be. She deserved that. In the meantime, I let her know that I loved her no matter what, with plenty of head pats and ear scratches. As I focused on Sadie's feelings, my own anxiety around her accidents eased. Sadie might have sensed this, because the more relaxed I was about her accidents, the less frequent they became.

She'd gone five whole days without one when I sat down to work on my Christmas Eve talk. Kevin was at work. Sadie lay at my feet, a stuffed gorilla nestled in her big puppy paws. I opened my Bible and skimmed the relevant verses. I flipped to John 1:14 and read, "The Word became flesh and made his dwelling among us."

I gazed at my contented puppy, who thrived on being in my presence. She needed to smell me. To lick me. To feel me pat her head and rub her tummy. To let me feed her twice a day. To hear me breathing next to her. My words were not enough. She needed to experience all of me to know she could trust me to be there for her, ready to care for her. Only then would something switch on like a neon sign inside her brain, a message that said: *I belong. I am wanted. I am loved.*

I started typing. I was not that different from my puppy. Words were not enough for me either. God knew that, so he gave me more. So much more. He sent Jesus at Christmas, not as an abstract belief, but as a baby who grew into a man. Jesus allowed people to see him. To feel his touch. To hear him speak. To know him. To learn to trust him. The more time I spent in God's presence, the stronger was my conviction: *I belong. I am wanted. I am loved.* God reminded me of those truths with a babe in a manger at Christmas. I stopped to text Kevin: "I'm working on my talk, inspired by you know who."

He replied with a doggie face emoji. Sadie leaned her weight against my leg. I pressed *save* on my computer. "Hey, good girl," I said, looking down at her. "Do you want to go for a walk?" ✹

THE JOY OF *god's grace*

Ruth's Reindeer Card

My young daughter had taken my joy to heaven with her. Not even Christmas could bring it back

by **MEADOW RUE MERRILL,** Richmond, Maine

WE WERE JUST back from the cut-your-own tree farm with a seven-foot Scotch pine. Dana, my husband, and our five kids paraded it through the house and fixed it in a stand in the family room. I put on holiday music and poured eggnog for everyone. Soon the tree would be aglow with lights. I sat on the couch with my eggnog, feeling lost in my own home. I wanted to join in the fun, but all I felt was sadness on my first Christmas without Ruth. She'd loved Christmas more than anything.

Ten months earlier, our seven-year-old daughter Ruth had died in her sleep from complications related to cerebral palsy. Her death was completely unexpected. Shattering. Despite the challenges of caring for a child who couldn't walk, couldn't talk, couldn't use her hands, we received one thing above all else from Ruth. She filled our lives with joy. Now, she'd gone to heaven and taken my joy with her. Not even Christmas could bring it back.

Born prematurely in a Ugandan hospital, Ruth had been abandoned by her mother and placed in a children's home. When Ruth failed to reach developmental milestones after her first birthday, the home's director was able to secure six months of specialized therapy for her at a facility in Maine. Friends of ours volunteered to host her.

One warm summer night in 2004, we visited our friends' church with our three children, all under the age of seven. There we met Ruth, who was just 19 days younger than our toddler. Ruth was much smaller in size and weight. She couldn't sit up or roll over, but when Dana moved her onto his lap, her face lit up. He raised a finger and wiggled it in the air. Ruth let out a delighted *hee-hee-hee* that made our kids laugh too. That was all it took. "Do you want to adopt her?" Dana asked.

We'd talked many times about adopting but never about adopting a child with disabilities. Especially while our children were so young. On our drive home, the kids couldn't stop talking about their new friend, Ruth. Neither could we.

We prayed for guidance, spent more time visiting with Ruth and really got to know her. We consulted doctors about her diagnosis. Eventually we became her new host family. The children welcomed Ruth into our home with open arms. The coming months were filled with fundraising, lawyers and a three-week trip to Uganda to complete the necessary paperwork. Then,

HAPPY FAMILY
Ruth (in red sweater) celebrates Christmas with her siblings.

the joys of Christmas 49

HEAVEN ON EARTH
Meadow and her husband, Dana (seated), with their ever-growing family

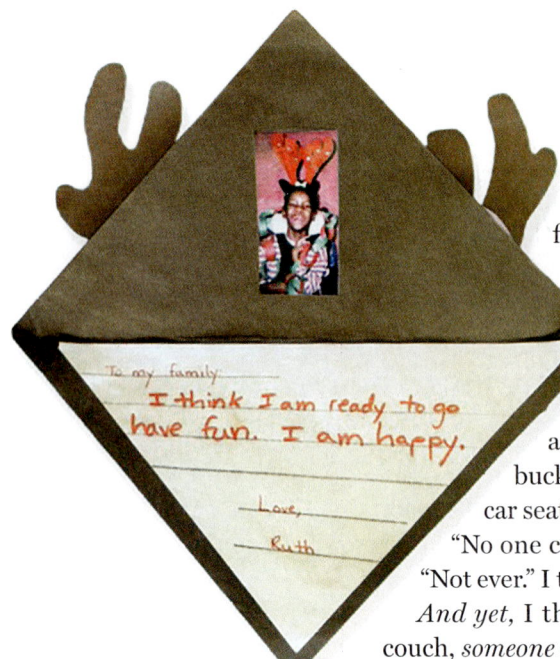

on Valentine's Day, February 14, 2006, a judge finalized Ruth's adoption at a little courthouse just down the road from our house.

"Do you know what this means?" I'd asked the children as Dana buckled their new sister in her car seat for the short drive home. "No one can take her away," I said. "Not ever." I truly believed that.

And yet, I thought, brooding on the couch, *someone had.* I hadn't touched my eggnog. "You're doing a wonderful job with the tree," I said to the children.

Ruth first attended a school for the deaf, where she thrived, communicating with an eye-gaze board. After memorizing the alphabet, she learned to pick out letters to spell words, including the names of everyone in our family. When Ruth turned six, she received a cochlear implant, a surgery that allowed her to hear. By first grade, Ruth understood spoken English so well she transferred to public school, where she quickly made a best friend and was learning to communicate using a computer.

Ruth's life was happy and full of love. She rarely cried, except when she suffered severe muscle spasms or when she thought someone else was hurt. Such as when the sheep in the movie *Babe* were attacked by mean dogs. I ran from the kitchen when I heard Ruth wail from her wheelchair in the living room. Only after I assured her that the movie on TV was just pretend did she stop crying.

Although Ruth needed assistance for daily living, she was as spirited as our other children. We considered her health to be as stable as all the rest.

That's why we were so horribly unprepared the dark February morning when Dana checked on Ruth in her bed and discovered that she'd stopped breathing. In the frantic minutes that followed, I called 911. Dana attempted CPR. But it was too late. "Sometimes with cerebral palsy, these things just happen," the doctor in the ER told us.

The days, weeks and months after were excruciating. Life felt hopeless. If God had led us to adopt Ruth, why had he taken her away? How could I ever find joy again for any reason?

I stared numbly at the tree. *I just want her back,* I told God for the millionth time. Nothing made sense. Including Christmas. Those glad tidings of great joy proclaimed by the angels seemed to be for other people. What was there for me to look forward to? Ruth wasn't coming back, and with her gone, I felt only the cold grip of despair.

Dana's eyes met mine. He could see that I was drifting to my dark place. He handed me a box of ornaments to try to engage me. To pull me back to our family still here with us. I tried to be present for our children. I knew they were hurting too, and I knew how sad that would have made their sister, Ruth.

I set down my eggnog and lifted the lid on the box. On top was a decoration I didn't recognize—a construction paper reindeer folded into a card.

Curious, I opened it. Glued inside was a photo of Ruth wearing a pair of light-up reindeer antlers. She was wrapped in a red-and-green paper chain, and she was grinning—that enormous smile I remembered so well. Blinking back tears, I read the neat letters printed inside, *"To my family, I think I am ready to go have fun. I am happy. Love, Ruth."*

"Look what I found!" I almost didn't recognize the thrill in my voice.

I held out the card. My husband and children gathered around. They were as surprised as I was when I showed them what was inside. Ruth must have made the card in school the year before, her final Christmas. I imagined her picking the letters on her eye-gaze board as an aide carefully wrote down each one when prompted. How the card had found its way into the box without any of us seeing it, none of us knew. It was a mystery.

We passed around the paper reindeer, everybody wanting to hold the card in their hands and look at Ruth up close. She was the picture of joy. It was almost as if she had come back, just for a moment, with a message to comfort us all. Perhaps Ruth truly was ready to go—even if I wasn't ready to let her.

It's been nearly 15 years since Ruth died. Of course there are times I ache for her still. But the years have also brought the comfort and joy the angels proclaimed on that first Christmas. I proclaim that same comfort and joy every year when I hang Ruth's reindeer card on our tree.

Because of Christ's birth, I know I will see Ruth again. That is worth celebrating. As is the way our family has continued to grow. Two-and-a-half years after losing Ruth, Dana and I welcomed our youngest son. Recently, we added two daughters-in-law and became foster parents to two young children. I have much to look forward to. It's not just the loss of my dear Ruth that marks my life, it turns out, but the love that continues to flow through it because of her. ✳

WHAT PRAYER CAN DO

"It's True"

FOR A LOT OF six-year-olds, Christmas Eve was the most exciting night of the year. But I tossed and turned in bed, unable to sleep for a different reason. I felt nervous and unsure, doubts flickering in my mind, like the blinking star on top of our tree. I couldn't enjoy Christmas the way a normal kid would. My thoughts wouldn't let me.

It had all started before the holidays, when a girl at school asked if I was a Christian. I'd heard the word, but I didn't really know what it meant beyond a commitment on Sunday mornings. We didn't talk about religion in my house. My parents had nothing to say about it one way or the other, at least not in front of me. "My family doesn't go to church," I said to my classmate, hoping that answered her question.

The girl drew her own conclusions. She told everyone in school that I didn't believe in God. That wasn't what I'd said, but her statement made me think. It was too much for a six-year-old to work through on her own with no one to turn to for guidance. I knew about prayer and angels. I knew that Jesus was born on Christmas Day. But did I know for certain that God was real? Did I believe? Really believe deep down in my heart that all of it was true? *God, how can I know?*

Questions danced in my head in the place of sugar plum fairies, and I turned over in my bed. Just then, a blinding white light filled my room. I squinted my eyes. *Mom?* I wondered. *Dad?* Had someone turned on the ceiling light? But this light was way brighter.

I sat up in the quiet while my eyes adjusted. A woman stood at the foot of my bed. A glow emanated from her as if from a life-size night-light. She lit up the room as if it were a movie set. Maybe I should have been afraid, but I wasn't. I felt nothing but comfort gazing at the white garment that floated in the air around her. I recognized her right away. She was an angel. That I knew for sure. Angels were everywhere at Christmastime, a favorite decoration. Only this one was real.

She waited a long moment before speaking. "It's true," she said.

Her message delivered, the angel faded away, and the night returned to my room. I lay back on my pillow to sleep. Morning was still hours away, but I'd already gotten the one thing I really wanted for Christmas. To know deep down in my heart that it was true.

—JEANNIE HUGHES, HURRICANE, WEST VIRGINIA

NEED PRAYER?
Join the OurPrayer community! Submit your prayer requests and pray for others at **ourprayer.org**.

THE JOY OF
Nostalgia

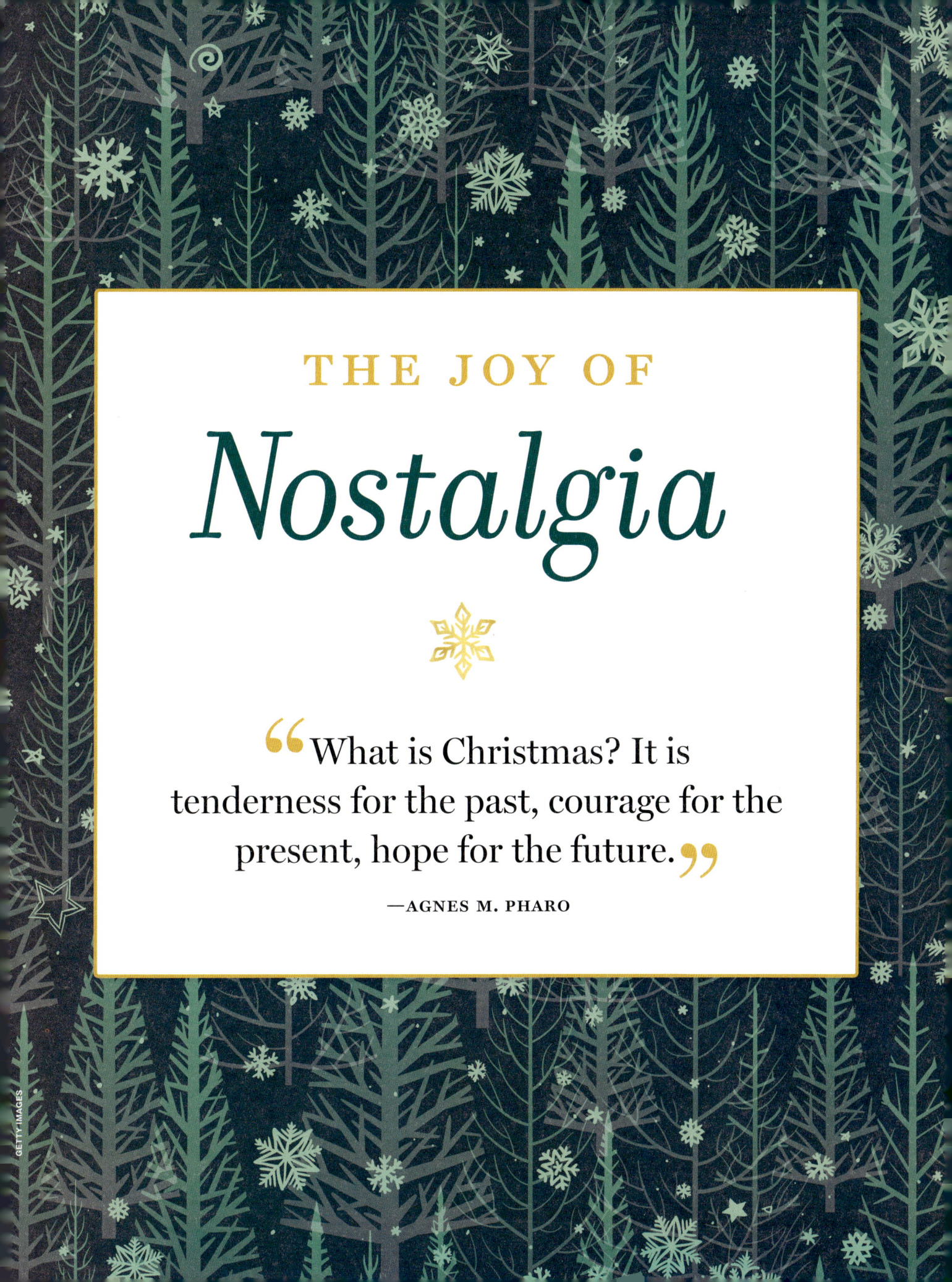

❄

"What is Christmas? It is tenderness for the past, courage for the present, hope for the future."

—AGNES M. PHARO

THE JOY OF *nostalgia*

Daddy took great pride in making sure the daily operations of the department store ran smoothly for employees and customers alike

After Hours

by **JENNIE IVEY**, Cookeville, Tennessee

Just as my family was finishing supper that Christmas Eve of 1968, the telephone rang. My mother got up to answer it. "Yes, he's here," she said, nodding toward my dad. "One moment." Dad pushed back his chair and made his way to the phone mounted on the wall beside the kitchen sink. Mother handed him the receiver.

"This is Ray Moore," Daddy said, stretching his back with his red hair mussed after a long day on his feet. "How can I help you?"

We watched Daddy's face fall with concern. He wrote something down on the notepad by the phone and then repeated what he'd written. Numbers. A phone number, I supposed. "Okay, I'll need to think this over for a few minutes," he said. "I'll call you back shortly."

Daddy returned to the table and pushed his last bite around the plate. The rest of us stared at him. My mother. My 11-year-old brother, Rusty. My sister, Mandy, age 2. And me, just a few days shy of 14.

"So…" Mother said, raising her eyebrows. "What was that all about?"

My dad was the manager of the Penneys department store at the 100 Oaks Mall in Nashville, Tennessee. It was the biggest Penneys in the southeastern United States, and Daddy took great pride in making sure the daily operations ran smoothly. He loved the hustle and bustle of the Christmas rush, but the oversight could be exhausting. Daddy spent his workday walking the floors of the two-level store, tending to the needs of employees and customers alike. Service was more personal back then, with paperwork done by hand. Many retailers offered a convenient layaway service. Shoppers could make a down payment on their purchases and then pay off the balance in installments over time. The store kept the items until they were fully paid for. Many people had to cut it close and couldn't make their final payments until Christmas Eve.

Like the man who had just called. "He found the store closed when he got there to retrieve his children's presents," Daddy told us. "He won't have any gifts to put under the tree on Christmas." The man had knocked on every door and window, hoping to catch the attention of a maintenance worker or guard. He'd finally copied Daddy's name and home number from a sign on the back door for emergencies only and called from a pay phone.

"I have to go back to the store and open up for him," Daddy said with a sigh. "What choice do I have?"

Mother had a ready answer for that. He had the choice to say no! Store hours were clearly posted. They were publicized in every newspaper and TV ad. The man had only himself to blame for the blunder. "You're worn out, Rayburn," she said.

"There is no reason you should have to reopen our Penneys this late on Christmas Eve. And in this nasty weather."

Daddy looked at Rusty and Mandy and me. "You kids go get ready for bed," he said. "You know Santa Claus will fly right on past our house without stopping if you're not sound asleep when he gets to Tennessee."

I lifted my sister out of her high chair. As we headed down the hall to our bedrooms, I asked Rusty to help Mandy brush her teeth and put on her pajamas. "I want to try to hear what they're saying," I whispered.

I got as close as I could without being detected. In a low but determined voice, Mother tried her best to convince Daddy to stay home. "You don't know a thing in the world about this man," she said. "He's clearly irresponsible. He might be drunk. Or a thief or con artist. This could be a plot to rob you and the whole Penneys store. Besides that, the weatherman is calling for sleet. The roads will be slick. You have no business out driving on a night like this, especially as tired as you are. And we've got our Santa job to do as soon as the kids are asleep."

I could picture Daddy standing by the phone, hands shoved deep into his pockets, trying to come to a decision. Then, softly, he spoke his mind: The man did not sound drunk, and most people, Daddy believed, were honest. "Just think about how excited our kids will be when they wake up tomorrow morning and find presents under the tree," he said. "How can I bear the thought that this man's children won't have any Christmas gifts at all because I'm holding them hostage at Penneys? That's no way to celebrate Jesus' birthday. Not for me or those kids."

I heard the receiver lift from its cradle. The rotary dial clicked around seven times. Daddy said he would meet the man at the back door of Penneys in half an hour. "I trust you're not lying to me, buddy," Daddy said. "Don't let me down."

KINDHEARTED MANAGER
Ray Moore risked a late-night return to work to ensure another family's happy Christmas.

PHOTOS COURTESY JENNIE IVEY

the joys of Christmas

REMEMBER WHEN *Jennie and her siblings, Mandy and Rusty, around the time of the story*

My siblings and I got into bed. Mother made the rounds, listening to prayers and kissing us good night. But try as I might, I couldn't fall asleep. I heard every sound in the house. Sleet pelted the windows as predicted. Mother paced the den floor. She turned on the TV, then turned it off again. *God, how can Daddy care so much about a family he doesn't even know?* I wondered.

The little bird in our cuckoo clock sang nine times. I got up and went to the den. "You're still awake?" Mother said. "Don't worry. Daddy will be home soon." But she didn't know I'd overheard all her wildest fears. We sat cross-legged on the floor in the glow of the Christmas tree and played gin rummy.

When headlights from the driveway shone through the window, I realized it had stopped sleeting. Mother hurried to the front door and pulled it open. In walked my daddy, as cheerful as could be. He rubbed his hands together to warm them and told us that the man had been waiting, as promised, at the back door of the store. "And the man was not the least bit drunk," Daddy noted for Mother's sake.

"It took me a while to find the paperwork for his layaway," Daddy said, "but I finally did. Wait till his children see their presents in the morning."

He'd helped the man load two shiny bicycles, a basketball and a dollhouse into the bed of a beat-up pickup truck. "He didn't shake my hand to thank me," Daddy said. "No, siree. He wrapped me in a big old bear hug and just about squeezed the breath out of me while he wished me merry Christmas over and over again."

I could see how much that meant to Daddy. He swept Mother and me into his arms and gave us a big old bear hug of our own. Then he winked at me and grinned like a red-headed Santa. "It's time you were in bed, Sister," he said. "I'm pretty sure I heard the jingle of reindeer bells as I pulled up to the house."

I didn't try to stay awake to get a glimpse of Santa's reindeer on the roof. I was content to have seen Daddy's headlights in the driveway. Because the honest and hardworking manager of a giant Penneys cared, another family would wake up to welcome Christmas just the way they'd hoped, with a joyful gathering around the tree. I realized Daddy *did* know that family he couldn't bear not to help. He knew them because they were just like us. ✶

56　GUIDEPOSTS

THE JOY OF *nostalgia*

Shared Memories

It seemed like everything I loved about Christmas was slipping away

by **NICKI COOPER,** Plano, Texas

EIGHT O'CLOCK Christmas morning, I pulled the shopping bag full of stocking stuffers out of my closet and crept down the hallway on tiptoe past the bedroom doors of my twin sons, Brennan and Breckan. *Why am I tiptoeing?* I asked myself. The "boys" were 20 years old and in college now, home on winter break. They'd stayed up late the night before playing video games, sharing new music they'd picked up at school, catching up with each other's lives (they went to school in different states), and Lord knows what else. I wasn't going to wake them if I tromped down the hall in combat boots. They'd sleep past the crack of noon if I didn't rouse them.

So why this concern with stealth? Maybe because I missed when the boys were little, and I secretly stuffed their stockings on Christmas Eve after they were fast asleep, making sure everything was just right for when they came racing down the hall in the morning, excited to see what Santa had left them.

They weren't boys anymore; they were young men. Too old to believe in Santa, too old to leave him cookies on our special "Cookies for Santa" plate, too old for the thank-you note Santa always left them. It seemed like everything I loved about Christmas was slipping away.

I prided myself on being a mom who remained well grounded. I'd raised my sons on my own after their father and I divorced when they were little. I'd taught middle school English for 27 years and moved heaven and earth to afford college tuition for Brennan and Breckan. I remembered once overhearing a coworker bemoan her son's leaving for college. I found myself thinking, *Get over it, lady. Your kid's growing up.* Now I was that mother.

Get over it, I chided myself as I filled the stockings with things that would be useful at college—phone chargers, travel-size items, disposable razors, mints and gum, gift cards from DoorDash and two pairs of goofy sunglasses. I was proud of the men Brennan and Breckan were becoming and eager to see where their lives would take them. But I just couldn't help myself from missing the little boys they were on those past Christmas mornings.

Something Breckan had said to me the day before he left for college his first year struck me now. I'd found him sitting in his

SUPERHEROES *Twins Breckan (Spiderman) and Brennan (Batman), age four, have a surprise for you-know-who.*

room instead of packing, looking gloomy. "You don't seem very excited about leaving for school tomorrow," I'd said, sitting down on the bed next to him.

Breckan looked up, almost tearful. "I want to stay here at home."

For just a second I felt a surge of guilty relief. "There's a community college not far away," I said. "You could start there, then transfer later if..."

Breckan shook his head. "No," he said. "I want to go to the University of Oklahoma. I just...I just want to stay here too."

I wrapped my arms around him. "I'm so proud of you and your brother. You'll be fine. You'll do great." *But would I?* I had wondered.

After the stockings were stuffed, I went to the kitchen to start our traditional Christmas cinnamon rolls breakfast. I rolled out the dough. When the boys were little, I helped them roll out the cookie dough. We would cut out reindeer shapes and pipe dots of red frosting onto their noses like Rudolph. We saved the best ones to leave out for Santa on his special plate. By morning, I'd have sampled the cookies myself and written a thank-you on Santa's behalf for the boys to find. How they loved those notes!

We had no time to bake cookies this year. There would definitely be no note from Santa. For the first time since I became a single mom, my parents hadn't spent the night with us on Christmas Eve. With two kids in college, I had a tight budget, and I'd rented out the guest room for extra money instead. Breckan considered his grandparents not being here on Christmas Eve a "bummer." To me, it was yet another bit of Christmas disappearing.

I shook my head as if I could shake away this yuletide melancholy. My sons didn't seem bothered to leave their childhood behind. They had their whole lives ahead of them. Could they possibly understand what I was feeling?

Okay, so they no longer left out cookies on Christmas Eve. So our "Cookies for Santa" plate had been stashed away for good. So I no longer wrote thank-you notes to them from Santa. They would make their own Christmas traditions with their own families one day.

I needed to see Christmas anew and not just as a mother lost in the past. *Help me, Lord, to find joy again in the miracle of your birth. You have given me so much to be happy about, especially on Christmas.*

When even the scent of freshly baked cinnamon rolls wasn't persuasive enough to rouse the twins, I went to get them up myself. I checked the stockings one more time before going upstairs. Something caught my eye. The cake stand that usually sat on the kitchen countertop was now on top of the bar that separated the kitchen from the living room. *What's that doing there?* I wondered.

I went to pick it up. The cake stand wasn't empty. Three Chips Ahoy! Reese's peanut butter cup cookies were arranged on it, uneaten. It took me a second to process what I was seeing.

Someone had left out cookies for Santa. In the middle of the night. No wonder the boys were still in bed!

I quickly stashed two of the cookies away and took a big bite out of the third. I grabbed a yellow legal pad from the countertop and a green marker and wrote, "Dear B and B, thanks for the cookies. I've been thinking you forgot about me. Sorry I couldn't finish them; I'm pretty full." I wiped away a tear before it splashed on the paper.

I left the note and the half-eaten cookie on the cake stand and went upstairs to

THE JOY OF *nostalgia*

wake the boys. "Merry Christmas, sleepyheads! Rise and shine!"

After my parents arrived, we all enjoyed the cinnamon rolls. No one cast a single glance at the cake stand. So when the plates were cleared away, I pretended to discover it myself.

"Hey, guys!" I said. "Santa left a note! Did one of you leave him cookies?"

"Who, us?" said Brennan. His brother gave a sly smile.

"You stinkers," I said.

They hadn't forgotten. Christmas is all about shared memories and the soft joy that they bring to our hearts when we gather to celebrate the birth of a savior. Maybe next year I won't feel the need to tiptoe at all. ✶

HOMECOMING *Last Christmas, Brennan (left) and Breckan's surprise was for their mom, Nicki.*

the joys of Christmas 59

THE JOY OF *nostalgia*

Three hauntingly beautiful stories of Christmases past
from the co-founder of GUIDEPOSTS, Norman Vincent Peale

I Remember...

SO IT COMES AGAIN, this marvelous Christmas season, the time of chimes and carols, of joy and wonder. A time of fond memories too, when people look back with love and longing to other Christmases.

There are three particular Christmases in my own past that had a special warmth for me. As everyone knows, gold and frankincense and myrrh were the first Christmas offerings. The gifts given to me on those three particular occasions were no less real. Each came unexpectedly—and each left me a changed person.

1 Some of my most impressionable boyhood years were spent in Cincinnati, Ohio. I still remember the huge Christmas tree in Fountain Square—the gleaming decorations, the streets ringing with the sound of carols. Up on East Liberty Street, where we lived, my mother always had a Christmas tree with real candles on it, magical candles that, combined with the fir tree, gave off a foresty aroma, unique and unforgettable.

The Christmas Eve when I was 12, I was out with my minister father doing some late Christmas shopping. He had me loaded down with packages, and I was tired and cross. I was thinking how good it would be to get home when a beggar—a bleary-eyed, unshaven, dirty old man—came up to me, touched my arm with a hand like a claw and asked for money. He was so repulsive that instinctively I recoiled.

Softly my father said, "Norman, it's Christmas Eve. You shouldn't treat a man that way."

I was unrepentant. "Dad," I said, "he's nothing but a bum."

My father stopped. "Maybe he hasn't made much of himself, but he's still a child of God." He then handed me a dollar—a lot of money for those days and for a preacher's income. "I want you to take this and give it to that man," he said. "Speak to him respectfully. Tell him you are giving it to him in Christ's name."

"Oh, Dad," I protested, "I can't do anything like that."

My father's voice was firm. "Go and do as I tell you."

So, reluctant and resisting, I ran after the old man and said, "Excuse me, sir. I give you this money in the name of Christ."

He stared at the dollar bill, then looked at me in utter amazement. A wonderful smile came to his face, a smile so full of life and beauty that I forgot that he was dirty

ILLUSTRATIONS BY SONIA PULIDO

60 GUIDEPOSTS

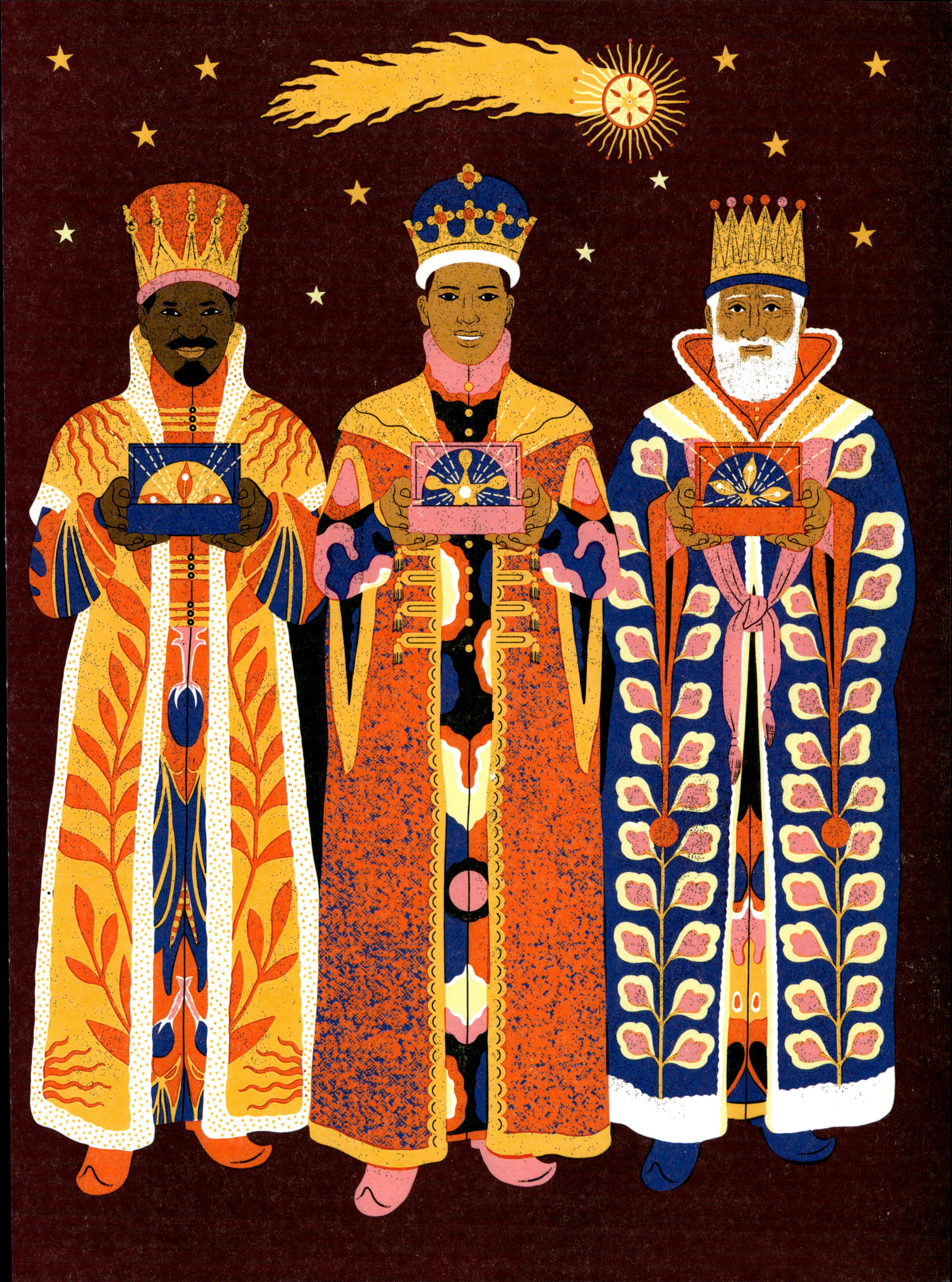

and unshaven. I forgot that he was ragged and old. With a gesture that was almost courtly, he took off his hat. Graciously he said, "And I thank you, young sir, in the name of Christ."

All my irritation, all my annoyance faded away. The street, the houses, everything around me suddenly seemed beautiful because I had been part of a miracle that I have seen many times since—the transformation that comes over people when you think of them as children of God, when you offer them love in the name of a baby born two thousand years ago in a stable in Bethlehem, a person who still lives and walks with us and makes his presence known.

That was my Christmas discovery that year—the gold of human dignity that lies hidden in every living soul, waiting to shine through if only we'll give it a chance.

2 The telephone call to my father came late at night and from a most unlikely place—a house in the red-light district of the city. The woman who ran the house said that one of the girls who worked there was very ill, perhaps dying. The girl was calling for a minister. Somehow the woman had heard of my father. Would he come?

My father never failed to respond to such an appeal. Quietly he explained to my mother where he was going. Then his eyes fell upon me. "Get your coat, Norman," he said. "I want you to come too."

My mother was aghast. "You don't mean you'd take a 15-year-old boy into a place like that!"

My father said, "There's a lot of sin and sadness and despair in human life. Norman can't be shielded from it forever."

We walked through the snowy streets, and I remember how the Christmas trees glowed and winked in the darkness. We came to the place, a big old frame house. A woman opened the door and led us to an upstairs room. There, lying in a big brass bed, was a pathetic, doll-like young girl, so ashen and frail that she seemed like a child, scarcely older than I was.

Before he became a minister, my father had been a physician, and he knew the girl was gravely ill. When he sat on the edge of the bed, the girl reached for his hand. She whispered that she had come from a good Christian home and was sorry for the things she had done and the life she had led. She said she knew she was dying and that she was afraid. "I've been so bad," she said. "So bad."

I stood there listening. I didn't know what anybody could do to help her. But my father knew. He put both his big, strong hands around her small one. He said, "There is no such thing as a bad girl. There are girls who act badly sometimes, but there are no bad girls—or bad boys either—because God made them and he makes all things good. Do you believe in Jesus?" The girl nodded. He continued, "Then let me hear you say, 'Dear Jesus, forgive me for my sins.'" She repeated those words. "Now," he said, "God loves you, his child who has strayed, and he has forgiven you, and no matter when the time comes, he will take you to your heavenly home."

If I live to be a hundred, I will never forget the feeling of power and glory that came into that room as my father then prayed for that dying girl. There were tears on the faces of the other women standing there, and on my own too, because everything sordid, everything corrupt was simply swept away. There was beauty in that place of sin. The love born in Bethlehem was revealing itself again on a dark and dismal street in Cincinnati, and nothing could withstand it. Nothing.

So that was the gift I received that Christmas, the frankincense-knowledge that there is good in all people, even the sad and the forlorn, and that no one need be lost because of past mistakes.

3 It was Christmas Eve in Brooklyn. I was feeling happy because things were going well with my church. As a young bachelor minister, I had just had a fine visit with some parishioners and was saying goodbye to them on their porch.

All around us houses were decorated in honor of Christ's birthday. Suddenly a pair of wreaths on the house across the street caught my eye. One had the traditional red bow, bright and cheery. But the ribbon on the other was a somber black—the symbol of a death in the family, a funeral wreath.

Something about that unexpected juxtaposition of joy and sorrow made a strange impression on me. I asked my host about it. He said that a couple with small children lived in the house, but he did not know them. They were new in the neighborhood.

I said good night and walked down the street. But before I had gone far, something made me turn back. I did not know those people either. But it was Christmas Eve, and if there was joy or suffering to be shared, my calling was to share it.

Hesitantly I went up to the door and rang the bell. A tall young man opened the door. I told him that I was a minister whose church was in the neighborhood. I had seen the wreaths, I said, and wanted to offer my sympathy. "Come in," he said quietly.

The house seemed very still. In the living room, a coal fire was burning. In the center of the room was a small casket. In it was the body of a little girl about six years old. I can see her yet, lying there in a pretty white dress, ironed fresh and clean. Nearby was an empty chair where the young man had been sitting, keeping watch beside the body of his child.

I was so moved that I could barely speak. *What a Christmas Eve,* I thought. Alone in a new neighborhood, no friends or relatives, a crushing loss. The young man seemed to read my thoughts. "It's all right," he said, as if he were reassuring me. "She's with the Lord, you know." His wife, he said, was upstairs with their two other children. He took me to meet them.

The young mother was reading to two small boys. She had a lovely face, sad yet serene. And suddenly I knew why this little family had been able to hang two wreaths on the door, one signifying life, the other death. They had been able to do it because they knew it was all one process, all part of God's wonderful and merciful and perfect plan for all of us.

They had heard the great promise that underlies Christmas: "Because I live, ye shall live also" (John 14:19). They had heard it, and they believed it. That was why they could move forward together with love and dignity, courage and acceptance.

So that was the gift I received that year, the reaffirmation that the myrrh in the Christmas story is not just a reminder of death but also a symbol of the love that triumphs over death.

The young couple asked if they could join my church. They did. We became good friends. Many years passed, but not one went by without a Christmas card from some member of that family expressing love and gratitude. But I was the one who was forever grateful. ✺

the joys of Christmas

THE JOY OF *nostalgia*

Guests at the Barn

Playing hide-and-seek was one thing. Christmas dinner was another. Would we eat with the cows and chickens?

by **ISABEL WOLSELEY TORREY,** Wilsonville, Oregon

READER FAVORITE

IMPOSSIBLE! That is what my mother said about the upcoming Christmas family reunion. It was our turn to host. "How can I fit over 50 people into this house?" In my bedroom, I looked up from reading about Dick Tracy and his two-way wrist radio. There wasn't a conversation that went on without the whole house hearing. The place was tiny. It looked like a dollhouse beside our big barn. I tried to count up the family members who would be coming. There was Mom, Dad, me and my little sister, Rosalie. Mom's six brothers and sisters. Their children—one of my uncles had 11 kids, another had 9. Some of them had children of their own. I didn't have to do the math to know Mom was right. They'd never fit in this house.

I turned the page of my comic and stared in shock at an ad showing that scandalous new bathing suit: a *bikini!* Then Mom's voice came again from the kitchen. "We can't afford a rental hall," she said.

"I'll come up with something," said Dad. That was his standard response to everything. But he didn't sound too sure of himself this time.

A couple of days later, Dad came up with his solution. "There's plenty of room in the barn," he told Mom after dinner.

"The *barn*?" Mom said.

Even I had to gasp. I loved our big barn. It was great for playing hide-and-seek or reading. Dad had hung a rope from the ceiling so we could swing from the hay bales. When I hit the highest point of my swing, I swear I could see all the way to France out the barn windows!

But swinging was one thing, Christmas dinner was another. Would we eat with the chickens? Sit in the cow stalls? Have Christmas in a barn?

"We'll borrow the church's folding tables and chairs for the adults," Dad said. "The kids can sit on the hay bales. I'll move the tractor and the corn-sheller outside for more space."

"Just make sure everyone knows it wasn't *my* idea!" Mom said. Then she thought of something else. "It could be freezing on Christmas Eve. How will we heat the fine venue?"

Dad scratched his head. "I'll come up with something." I couldn't help but root for him to find a solution.

Days passed. Then one afternoon, out of the blue, Dad found the answer. "Do you remember that old woodstove you wanted to get rid of?"

"Yes," said Mom. "The one you insisted on storing in the cellar."

ILLUSTRATION BY STELLA SWAN

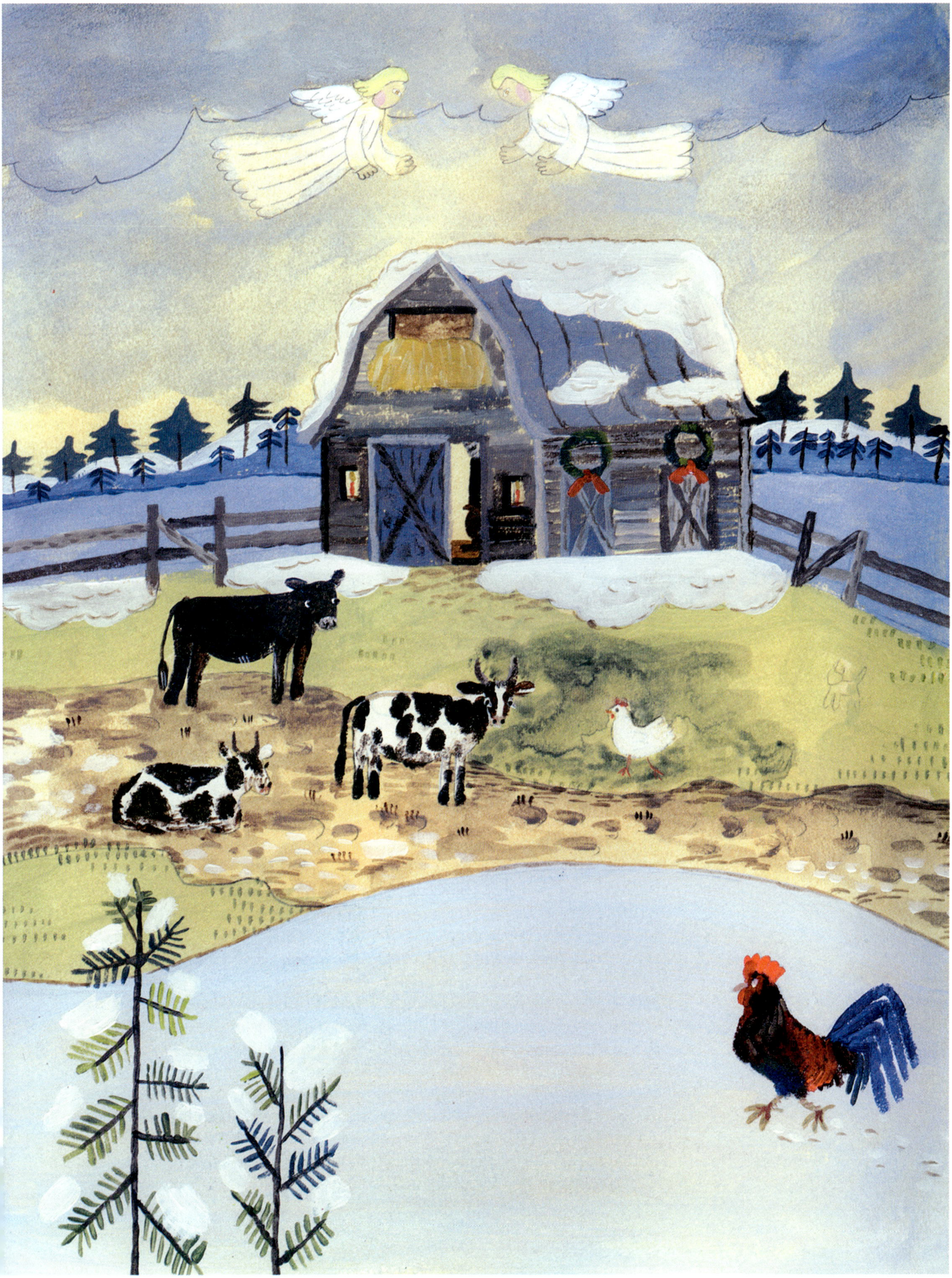

"We'll put it in the barn," Dad said. "The almanac says we're due for a mild Christmas. We'll be fine."

Mom marked the days till the reunion on the Purina Feed calendar. Over the coming weeks, we got the barn into shape. Mom broom-brushed the cobwebbed walls. Rosalie and I swept hay and dust off the concrete floor. Dad "neated up" the cow stalls. Some farmer neighbors helped Dad carry the stove to the barn, stick its exhaust pipe through a window and stock firewood by its side.

A few days before Christmas, we unfolded the church tables and chairs, spread a festive tablecloth, laid all the places. Dad lit

> *If we were just entertaining angels for Christmas, they could have fit in our tiny house.*

the woodstove to see how it worked. It didn't take long for the drafty barn to feel warm and cozy. What's more, the front of the stove had a little window made of isinglass. Through it, I could see the fire inside, casting a warm, beautiful glow. It was like having a real fireplace right there in the barn.

"We're ready," Mom said. Even she had faith in Dad's plan now.

The next day a wicked north wind roared across the Kansas plains, whipping up snow everywhere. Highway 50's black-licorice asphalt turned white. Black ice crusted the road. Icicles hung from the phone lines and sparkled in the cornfields.

"What if nobody can get here?" I asked my parents. I no longer felt embarrassed about our Christmas barn dinner.

"Angels sang at Jesus' first birthday," said Dad. "They'll come to this one and pave the way for our guests."

I couldn't help thinking that if we were just entertaining angels for Christmas, they could have fit in our tiny house. But Dad was right. By the time the rooster crowed on the day of the reunion, the sky had cleared. We were just finishing breakfast when a noise like a coffee grinder split the early morning silence. It was a truck, slip-sliding its way up the lane to our house. My uncle Elmer popped his head out. "Betcha thought we wouldn't make it clear from Wichita!" he called.

Aunt Sadie climbed out. "Where do I put the fried chicken?"

We led the way into the barn, followed by Uncle Elmer, Aunt Sadie and the eight kids they'd crammed into the backseat. "Neat!" they said when they saw our pot-bellied stove.

Pickup trucks arrived all day, with more relatives and more food. I ran from the house to the barn and back again, eagerly listening to everyone catching up.

"I put up a hundred quarts of tomatoes this year," Aunt Minnie told the other women in the kitchen.

"Heard the Millers got 30 bushels per acre," Uncle Jack was saying to the men by the corral fence.

"Isabel, come and play hide-and-seek!" my cousins called from the haymow.

At dinnertime, Mom clanged the cowbell hanging from its strap by the haymow ladder. "Come and get it!"

We took our places on folding chairs and hay bales. Grandpa read the Twenty-Third Psalm from the Bible and led us in a blessing. We ate, talked and laughed for so long, the cows started bawling to come in for milking. Dad opened the door and in they came, snorting steaming clouds of air all the way to their stalls.

I'd thought a barn was a strange place for Christmas dinner, but all this time later it remains my favorite setting. Because that year we had everything Jesus did on the first Christmas. We had family, hay, farm animals—and, of course, angels. ✶

THE JOY OF *nostalgia*

Just a Peek

The enchanting vintage ornaments hold miniature worlds

by **ROSE ROSS ZEDIKER,** Elk Point, South Dakota

THE CHRISTMAS EVE I was four years old, I was excited to be an angel in our church's living Nativity scene. I didn't mind that I couldn't see my parents and grandparents in the audience, but I couldn't get even a glimpse of Baby Jesus. The older boys playing the Three Wise Men stood directly in front of me. I tried peeking around the tall trio, but I had to elbow up beside them to get a better view. People in the audience chuckled.

At my grandparents' house that night, I sat on Grandpa's lap, craning my neck to search the branches of their tree for four colorful plastic teardrop-shaped ornaments, each open in the middle to display a tiny 3D diorama. I pointed to my favorite with the simplest Nativity scene inside.

"I just wanted to see Baby Jesus," I said. "I was embarrassed when people laughed."

Grandpa hugged me. "It's always good to keep your eyes on Jesus." It was all I needed to hear. That story became a family favorite. Grandpa repeated it every Christmas, and I grew up on his sage advice, loving the Jewelbrite ornaments all the more.

In 2004, I inherited the four my grandparents owned, but when I hung them on my tree, they looked out of place beside my modern Christmas ornaments. I decided to use the vintage baubles to decorate a tabletop tree instead. It was rare that I could add to my original set with a treasure found at a thrift or antique store. The unique ornaments, popular in the 1950s and '60s, hadn't been manufactured for decades and were greatly prized by collectors.

After a few Christmases with my tabletop tree, I ventured into a small-town antique shop. I gasped in delight at the sight of a full-size aluminum tree covered in nothing but Jewelbrites. So many shapes, colors and diorama scenes! I admired each one and chose 50 to buy.

"Forget my little tabletop tree," I told the clerk. "I'll have plenty to decorate our seven-foot fir!"

"The ornaments belonged to the store owner's aunt," the clerk said. "It wasn't easy to let them go, but downsizing was a must."

The story touched my heart. "Please tell the owner that they will be loved in my family as much as they were in hers."

And that proved true. My granddarlings ooh and aah over my Jewelbrites as much as I do. We can spend hours discovering some new detail in their miniature worlds. My youngest granddaughter told me last Christmas, "I love your ornaments because when you look at them, something peeks back at you."

Her remark summoned to mind that little girl who felt embarrassed when she got caught sneaking a peek at Baby Jesus way back when. Grandpa's words had made it all okay as I sat on his knee gazing in wonder at the baby cradled in my favorite ornament on the tree. Today I hang my Jewelbrites with Nativity dioramas front and center, right where Grandpa taught me to keep Jesus always. ✶

THE JOY OF *nostalgia*

Visitors to the Parsonage

His father preached at a small church in Ohio and took on side jobs so the family could get by

by **DANIEL SCHANTZ,** Moberly, Missouri

Growing up a preacher's kid in the 1940s and '50s, I knew the biblical Christmas story by heart and I loved it. Still, I was as caught up in the culture of Christmas as any other American child: cutting down the Christmas tree, caroling in town, eating rich holiday treats like fruitcake and pecan pie, and most of all, opening presents. Could there ever be enough presents under the tree? I was impatient to find out how many would have my name on the tag. Christmas was a "me-centered" holiday for most kids my age, and I was no different. All that changed the Christmas I was 13.

Once the tree was up that year, my mother sat us children around the table with the Sears catalog. "Pick your three favorite gifts," she said, "and number them from one to three." When it was my turn to look through the thick book, with its distinctive paper-and-ink smell, I saw many things I wanted—and even more we couldn't afford. I asked for an imitation leather stamp album for my collection of USA postage stamps, a pocketknife and a set of colored pencils, in that order. It was understood that we might not get all three items we'd chosen, but I secretly hoped that my parents would somehow find a way to give us more than what we asked for. To read our minds and know what wonderful things we really wanted. A boy could dream, after all.

I knew that my family was not well-to-do. My father preached at a small church in Ohio that couldn't pay a living wage. With six of us kids to feed and clothe, Mom had her hands full at home and Dad had to take on side jobs so we could get by. In between preparing sermons and making hospital calls, he often did farmwork, putting up hay and milking cows. When he filled in for the janitor at my school, I was both proud of him and somewhat ashamed that he was doing a job he wasn't trained for. His specialty was door-to-door selling. He sold Fuller Brush household cleaning supplies, Wear-Ever aluminum pots and pans and his favorite product of all: big family Bibles. He was a natural-born salesman, handsome and charming, with a million-dollar smile. Plus, everyone knew he was an honest man.

Our one big financial break of the year came at Christmastime, when church and community friends came by the parsonage to show their appreciation for Dad's faithfulness. Businessmen dropped off gift-boxed specialty foods and enormous fruit baskets. A farmer might bring an armload of beef or a couple of hams, perhaps a turkey or even venison. Ladies' groups marched in with handmade quilts and af-

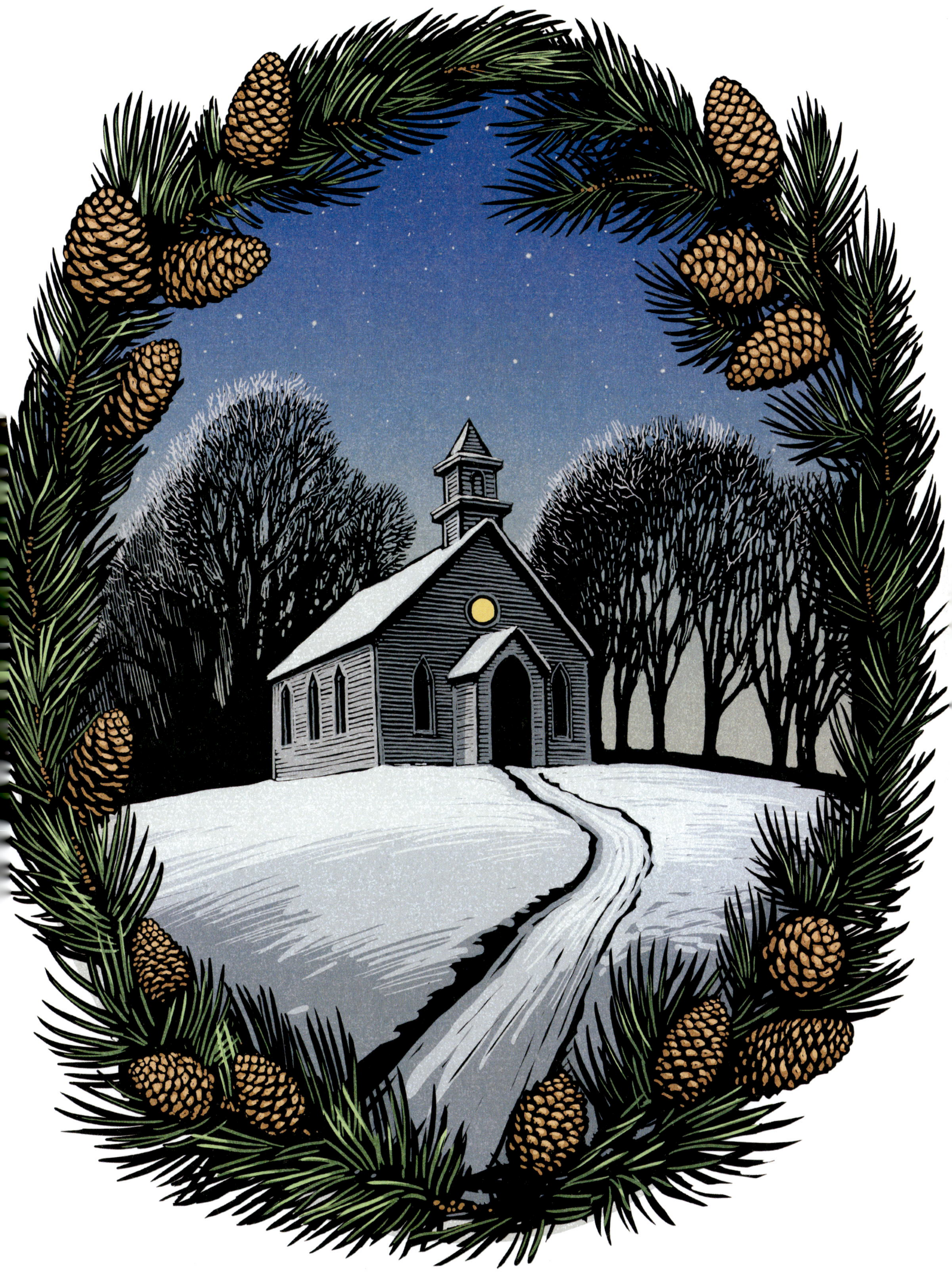

ghans and filled our pantry with canned goods. Shopkeepers offered Dad discounts on dress shirts and ties so he could spiff up his wardrobe for his official duties in the new year. A funeral director once brought him a bottle of wine, a box of cigars and a clever mechanical ashtray. Always gracious, my father accepted the trio of gifts with a smile. He didn't raise an eyebrow until he saw the man out and gave the ashtray to us kids to play with. It was one of our favorite "toys" that year. Grandmothers always remembered us children with games and hard tack candy. If the doorbell rang, there was usually a present behind it waiting to be opened.

However, people showed up at Christmastime for other reasons too. Some were lonely or sad or feeling the sting of having strayed from their faith at a time when everyone else seemed to be celebrating it. They came to talk to Dad, knowing they would find a godly minister who would be understanding and nonjudgmental.

One day during that Christmas I was 13, a loud knock at the parsonage door

> *That childish self-centeredness was crowded out by a consuming desire to be like my kind and generous father.*

brought a surprise the likes of which our family had never seen. A church member who was a big shot at the bank stopped by with a Christmas card he wanted to deliver personally. Dad opened the card to find a $50 bill inside. A lot of money! He shook the banker's hand with much gratitude. Dad was very pleased with that bill, holding it up for all of us to see, then sliding it into his pocket for safekeeping. I imagined it went a long way toward easing his mind as the breadwinner of our family. I also spent some time dreaming about what my parents could buy for me with it.

Later that evening a married couple appeared at our front door. I stood next to Dad while the young man explained that he'd lost his job, times were hard and something as simple as the Christmas spirit felt like a luxury. Dad invited the couple inside and directed them to the dining room for privacy. "I won't be too long," he said to me.

I waited just outside the doorway while Dad listened to the couple's story in detail. He spoke with them about putting their trust in God and quoted some comforting scriptures: "The Lord is my shepherd, I shall not want," "God is our refuge and strength, a very present help in time of trouble." I grew impatient, wishing he would hurry, as he had promised that we'd play a game of checkers by the tree.

Finally they all stood up from the dining room table. Dad put his arms around our visitors' shoulders and prayed. "Lord, here is a young couple who needs your help, just as Mary and Joseph once needed help. I pray that you will provide for them as only you can do and give them peace."

Then my father did something I'll never forget. He reached in his pocket, pulled out the $50 bill and pressed it into the young man's hand. I caught my breath. My eyes got wide. Dad put his finger to his lips and ushered the couple to the door, not even wanting a thank-you. He'd parted with the banker's gift without hesitation.

In that moment, time seemed to slow. I felt as patient as I had ever been. My holiday focus shifted from what I might find wrapped under the tree with my name on the tag. That childish self-centeredness was crowded out by a consuming desire to be like my kind and generous father. His quiet gesture had given me something to live up to. It was a priceless gift, better than any gift I could ever dream up, a gift as precious as a baby born in a manger. The year I was 13, Dad put Christmas in my heart. ✺

THE JOY OF *nostalgia*

All the Loving Reasons

The keepsake was now better than new

by **ALINE ALEXANDER NEWMAN,** Turin, New York

While trimming the tree with my grandchildren, I dropped my favorite ornament on our tiled family room floor. The ball broke into pieces. "Oh, God, why did it have to be this one?" I could have cried.

Ten-year-old Chase came over to see what had me so upset. He stooped down with me and picked up the ornament's metal cap. "Was it a special one?" he wanted to know.

"A collectible," I said. I explained that it was a treasured souvenir from a long-ago trip his grandpa and I had taken to the Norman Rockwell Museum in Stockbridge, Massachusetts. The ornament featured a rhyme I knew by heart—"Christmas time is filled with joy and glad anticipation. And all the loving reasons for a happy celebration"—plus three of Rockwell's beloved Christmas scenes. Rockwell's name meant nothing to young Chase, of course, but he gave me a hug.

"Never mind," I said, feigning a cheerful tone. "Forget that, and let's finish decorating this tree." Chase rejoined the others, but I couldn't let go of my disappointment just yet.

Norman Rockwell was my favorite illustrator. Thin, gawky and completely unathletic, he dropped out of high school at age 16 and enrolled in The National Academy of Design. So good was he that he was appointed art editor of the Boy Scout magazine, *Boys' Life*, when he was only 19. Three years later, he began painting for the *Saturday Evening Post*. His first Christmas cover, for the December 1916 issue, was a delight. Called "Playing Santa," the illustration featured an old man in a store, trying on a long white beard. In 47 years with the *Post*, Rockwell painted an astonishing 332 covers and countless inside pages.

Whatever the assignment, Rockwell's approach was unique. He started by imag-

ON SANTA'S NICE LIST
Aline and her grandson, Chase

the joys of Christmas

THE JOY OF *nostalgia*

ining a homey, often gently humorous, scene drawn from everyday American life. Then he selected real people from among his family, neighbors and friends to act as models for his characters. Sometimes he went on location, but most often he collected props that he set up in his studio. Only after all that would he paint, capturing every detail.

When I was growing up, my maternal grandparents lived on the next block, and I

> *I mourned my broken ornament, with its endearing Christmas scenes and the memories it brought up for me.*

often walked over to their house after school. Their magazine subscriptions would pile up, and my grandfather and I sat side by side entertaining ourselves with Rockwell's *Saturday Evening Post* illustrations. Years later, my favorite aunt gave my parents a wonderful Christmas present, a copy of Christopher Finch's coffee table book, *332 Magazine Covers—Norman Rockwell*. I was married by then but lived close enough to my parents that I could indulge in a favorite childhood pastime, poring over the unwieldy gift that weighed more than 10 pounds.

The coffee table book introduced me to Rockwell's later work for *Look* magazine. There, Rockwell often took a more serious tone. He used his talents to promote important American causes, such as the struggle for civil rights, the war on poverty and the nation's space program.

Not only were Rockwell's illustrations extremely realistic and beautifully rendered, but so many of them also told a story. For example, "Bringing Home the Tree," one of the paintings on my broken ornament, depicted a satisfied-looking man carrying an evergreen tree over his shoulder. Accompanying him were three frolicking dogs and a boy carrying the ax that had gotten the job done. Father and son, no doubt, walking in lockstep. But I could see much more than that. I envisioned the father and son traipsing into the woods, finding the perfect tree, chopping it down and taking it home to Mom, who made them hot cocoa for their efforts. I mourned my broken ornament, with its endearing Christmas scenes and the memories it brought up for me.

Meanwhile, the living room where I stood lost in thought was bustling. I looked over to see that our tree had been fully decorated while I was musing.

Chase ran to my side. "Here, Grandma," he said, handing me something round. "I fixed it."

I could see the paper towel stuffed inside the ball he'd taped and wrapped with rubber bands that somehow held the metal cap on top again. A straightened paper clip served as a hanger. Tears sprang to my eyes.

"You're a wonder," I said. Chase beamed. The scene might have been staged by Norman Rockwell himself, but the lovingly cobbled-together ornament reminded me never to get so caught up in the past that I overlook the wonderful things God has put right in front of me. ✴

TREASURES UNTOLD
The restored Norman Rockwell collectible

THE JOY OF
Cranberries

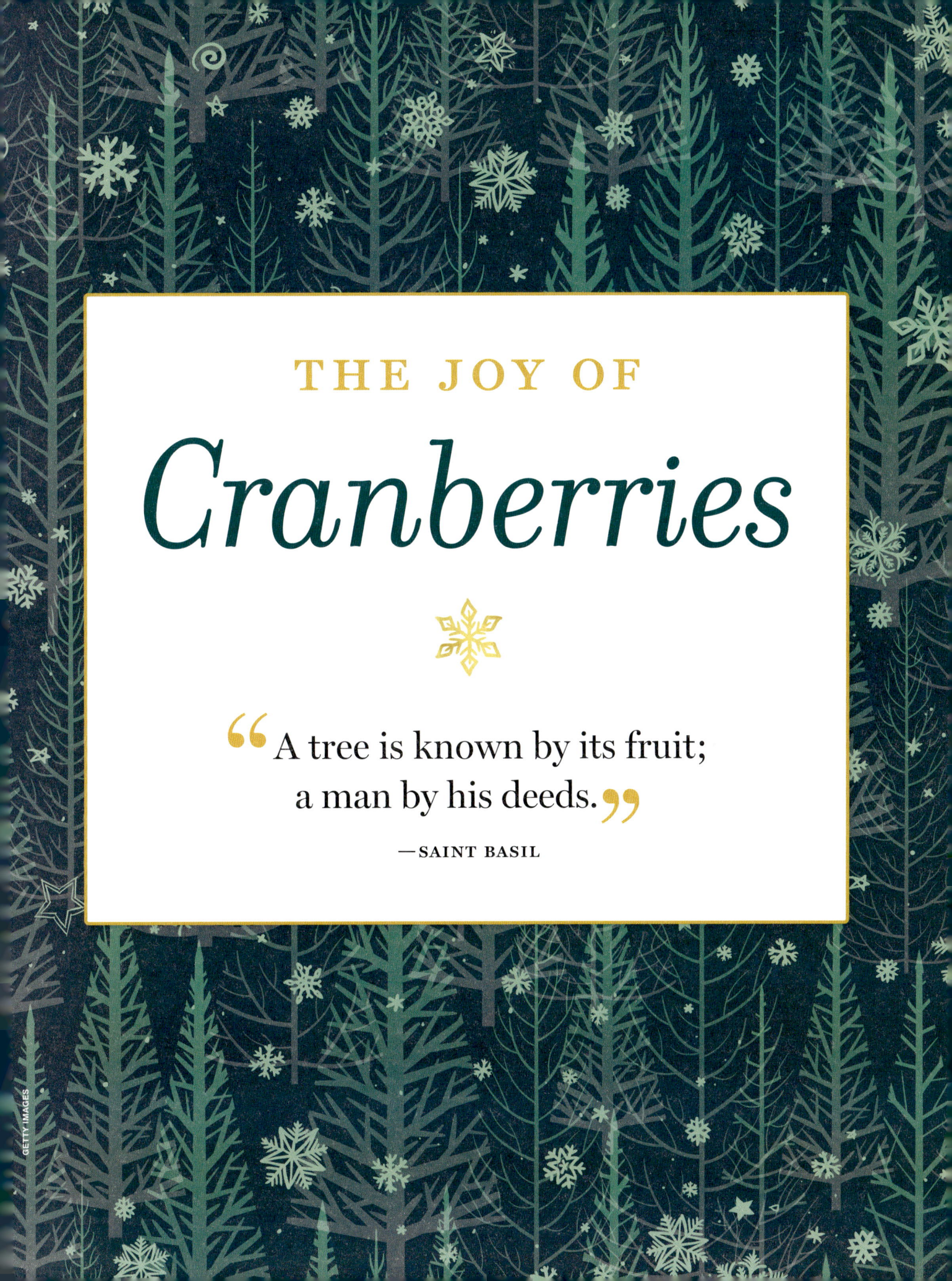

"A tree is known by its fruit; a man by his deeds."

—SAINT BASIL

THE JOY OF *cranberries*

Kitchen Time

An award-winning baker has a second "family room" in her house

by **WHITNEY MILLER,** Spring Hill, Tennessee

My best childhood Christmas memories involve the kitchen. Mom was an elementary school teacher, Dad was a basketball coach, and my two sisters and I had them running in all directions with our extracurricular activities. But during holiday breaks, our family was very intentional about spending time together in our favorite room of the house—the kitchen.

Especially on Christmas morning. As soon as presents were opened, Dad would announce, "Time to make breakfast!" We'd all pile into the kitchen to make biscuits, pancakes, bacon, eggs and grits. Why choose? After the big morning meal, there was no need for lunch...which was helpful because we'd spend the rest of the day preparing Christmas dinner.

In addition to the ham, turkey and traditional sides, we made all manner of sweets. I don't think a store-bought dessert ever found its way into our home. Mom always made baking fun for us, channeling our energy into something creative without a care for the mess. I still have vivid memories of a cloud of cocoa powder settling onto my eyelashes when I couldn't resist peeking into the mixing bowl while someone added a heaping tablespoonful to the batter.

When my husband and I started a family, I wanted to make Christmas kitchen memories with our kids too. As a professional baker, I'm always experimenting, and my sons were used to watching Mommy "work." Once they turned six and four, I figured they were ready to get their little hands sticky from more than just eating. I came up with Christmas Chocolate Bark, a candy recipe with lots for them to do.

The boys stirred the chocolate until it was smooth and spread it onto a pan. I assigned them each an area they could take ownership of by sprinkling on the toppings of their choice. They crinkled their noses at the gold salt I wanted to use for a festive touch, until I suggested it would make the creation look like pirate treasure. They might have been too young to appreciate how salt brings out the chocolate's sweetness, but they were totally down for anything pirate adjacent!

There were times I had to call upon the patience Mom had modeled for me, but the boys were actually pretty good about taking turns. For those times when they just couldn't resist licking the spoon, I made a strong distinction between which batches were for gifts and which were strictly for our family. I also set aside a bowl of dried cranberries for nibbling to keep our measured ingredients from "disappearing."

Once the chocolate was set, the boys dis-

SWEET 'N' SALTY
Cranberries lend a pop of color to the Christmas Chocolate Bark, making it a cheery gift.

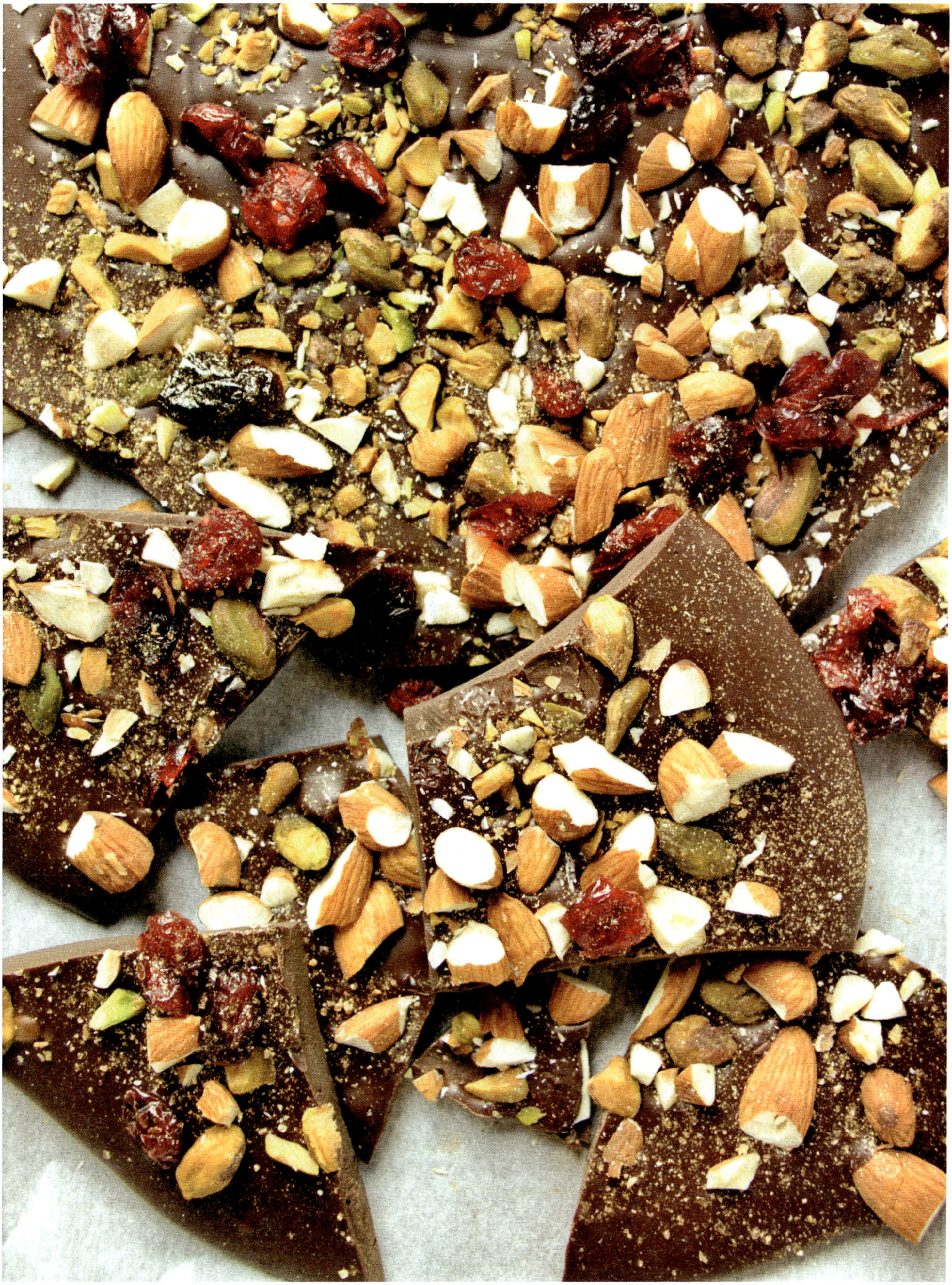

covered their favorite part of all: breaking the bark into pieces. The great thing about this recipe is that the broken pieces don't have to be uniform—in fact, it's prettier when they're not. The cranberries stand out so beautifully against the dark background, and the mixture of crunchy and smooth, sweet and salty gives this simple confection a wonderful depth. The recipe can be altered to suit different tastes, so the sprinkling ingredients are suggestions more than hard-and-fast rules. However, I do think the red cranberries and gold salt take the presentation up a notch.

The boys were so proud to give out their boxes of Christmas Chocolate Bark, especially when someone would ask, "You made this yourself? It looks like it came from a fancy store!" Soon, our little girl, who will be two this Christmas, will be old enough to take part with her brothers, now eight and six. For me, there's nothing that comes out of our kitchen sweeter than the time our family spends in it together. ✳

KID-FRIENDLY *Whitney came up with Christmas Chocolate Bark as a confection her children could help make.*

Christmas Chocolate Bark

- 2 (10-ounce) bags 60% to 70% cacao bittersweet or dark chocolate chips
- ½ cup toasted almonds
- ¼ cup toasted pistachios
- ⅓ cup sweetened dried cranberries and/or cherries
- Flaky sea salt (optional)

Place the chocolate chips in a large microwave-safe bowl. Melt the chocolate in the microwave in 30-second increments, stirring after each one. Stop microwaving when the chocolate is about 90% melted. Stir until all the chocolate is melted and smooth.

Line a baking sheet with parchment paper. Pour the melted chocolate in the middle of the baking sheet. Using a rubber spatula, evenly spread the chocolate until it is ¼ to ⅛ inch thick.

Roughly chop the toasted almonds and pistachios. Evenly sprinkle the nuts and dried fruit over the melted chocolate. If desired, crush flaky sea salt over the chocolate.

Allow the chocolate to cool completely at room temperature for 2 to 4 hours. You can also refrigerate the chocolate bark for 30 minutes to an hour, or until set. (If refrigerated, the chocolate may discolor some.)

Once the chocolate is completely hardened, break the chocolate into pieces. Package the chocolate bark for gifting, or store in a container with a cover for up to 1 week.

Makes about 40 pieces.

THE JOY OF *cranberries*

Book Club Recs

Plenty of great novels to read, only one dish to serve

by **CITA SMITH,** Tuscaloosa, Alabama

"CITA, YOU MUST BRING your Cran-Apple Bake!" The ladies in my book club had been talking about novels once a month for at least three decades, and they always made the same request for our December gathering. But the recipe wasn't really mine at all.

At the school where I taught for nearly 40 years, the parents held a luncheon for the teachers just before holiday break. The mother of one of my students brought in a dish I fell in love with at first glance. It was bubbled around the edges, with chopped apples and vibrant red cranberries inside, some slightly burst from baking. The filling spilled out around the serving spoon. Chopped pecans nestled in brown sugar and toasted oatmeal graced the top. I was an English teacher, and I loved words. But the only thing I could say was "Ooh!" After a taste of the still-warm treat, I only repeated myself. The sweet and buttery crumble added a delightful contrast to the tart filling, so the dish was both crunchy and moist. The mom gladly shared the recipe when I could finally get the words out to ask her for it. I served it to my book club friends that very same December.

They raved. They had seconds. They oohed as I did. "Can you believe how delicious Cita's Cran-Apple Bake is?" they said. I felt sheepish about getting all the glory when I distinctly told everyone it was not my recipe. Nevertheless, the name stuck in our circle. A circle that only got wider when my friends passed the recipe on to their friends, just as they would pass on a good book. Trying to calculate how many Christmas tables must now include Cran-Apple Bake… well, it reminds me why I taught English instead of math!

I warn you that if you make this dish for your family and friends, you should plan on making it every Christmas for the rest of your life. I hope that "my" recipe becomes yours. ✳

Cran-Apple Bake

FILLING
- 2 cups fresh cranberries, washed
- 3 cups Rome apples, unpeeled, washed and cut into small pieces
- 1 cup sugar

Arrange the filling ingredients in the bottom of a lightly greased (or sprayed) 9x13-inch baking dish.

TOPPING
- 1 cup oatmeal
- 1 cup chopped pecans
- ½ cup brown sugar
- 1 cup melted butter or margarine

In a bowl, mix the topping ingredients together, then spread it over the fruit. Bake uncovered at 350°F until bubbly, about 45 minutes.

Serves 12.

THE JOY OF *cranberries*

A Bowl of *Brightness*

The beloved *Today* show weatherman, cohost and cook shares his must-have cranberry side dish

by **AL ROKER,** New York, New York

THERE ARE TWO camps when it comes to cranberry sauce. Are you Team Canned Cranberry? Or do you prefer homemade? I like both. There's something about the tradition of the ridged, berry-red, gelatinous cylinder popping out of the can, making a satisfying *sloop* sound when it lands on a serving dish, that just belongs to the holidays in my mind. But a fresh cranberry sauce—or relish? That's on a whole different level for my family and me.

Our Roker cranberry tradition actually started with a dear friend of ours, Carl Killingsworth. One Thanksgiving in the late 1990s, Carl said he'd bring the cranberry sauce. Well, he showed up at my door with the makings for what he called a cranberry relish—a bag of cranberries, a whole orange, some onion and sugar—and asked if he could use my food processor. I mean, listen, I don't let just anybody in my kitchen to cook, but when it's family or good friends, and they say, "Can I make this?" Sure. Come on over and help yourself. Carl did.

The smell of the cranberries and citrus mixing together was delightful. When I tasted the finished product, *whoa!* The relish was bright and tart and not anything like the smooth canned stuff or the whole-berry sauce. There's a world of difference in taste and texture. In the years since, I've even turned it into more of a dip by adding jalapeños and chopped-up tomatillos. It holds up with crackers and tortilla chips and complements cheeses. The key is to make the relish a day or two ahead of time. The more it sits, the better it gets. The sugar kind of macerates everything, and the flavors really come together.

Fresh Cranberry Relish

- **1** (12-ounce) bag fresh cranberries
- **1** whole orange, unpeeled, cut into eighths
- **½** small sweet onion, such as a Vidalia, peeled (optional)
- **½–1** cup sugar
- **Salt**
- **Freshly ground pepper**

Combine the cranberries, orange sections, onion (if using) and ½ cup of the sugar in a food processor. Process until finely chopped. Taste and add up to ½ cup more sugar, if desired. Season with salt and pepper. Transfer the relish to a bowl, and refrigerate for at least 1 day and up to 2 days before serving.
Makes 2½ cups.

We've got a pretty traditional Christmas menu in our house: turkey, ham, stuffing, collard greens, peas and rice. Mostly heavy dishes. So this cheerful little side is sort of a reset for your palate. It looks great on the table too. The orange from the fruit and deep maroon from the cranberries pop on the plate.

On Christmas morning, before the real cooking starts, you'll usually find us having breakfast in matching pj's. That started when our son, Nick, was about 10. He's 23 now. These days, it's a race between my wife, Deborah, and me to see who can find all the sizes in one pattern and order the pajama sets first. We don't consult with each other either. We have a winner when the "other half" finds an early Christmas delivery on our doorstep. The surprise can make me feel like a kid again.

When I was growing up, my mom was the magic behind every holiday meal. You didn't really see her cook. It just happened. She was in constant motion, somehow managing to time everything perfectly. I still don't know how she did it. That's the magic of mothers.

My dad never tired of making me feel loved too. One Christmas I caught the mumps and had to be quarantined. I must have been about eight years old. While I was asleep on Christmas Eve, Dad managed to move the whole tree, ornaments and all, into my room. I'll never forget the smile that put across my swollen cheeks when I woke up.

I think about those moments while preparing this recipe. The relish is first on my list before tackling the other dishes. (Remember, it's best to have it rest in the fridge for a while.) You put so much into holiday planning, from the timing of get-togethers to the food on the table to the gifts under the tree, and then it's all over. Except for the memories that will outlast any meal.

Cranberry relish isn't something I think about during the other 10 months of the year, but come November and December, this bowl of brightness is a must-have. Just open our fridge, and you'll see. ✺

CHRISTMAS MORNING
The Roker family enjoys a festive breakfast in their Snoopy pj's.

the joys of Christmas

THE JOY OF *cranberries*

Slice of Life

This easy recipe takes me right back to Grandma's elegant holiday table

by **JESSICA MERCHANT,** Irwin, Pennsylvania

MY DAD'S MOTHER was my favorite person in the whole world. A minimalist before it was chic, Grandma was the original queen of paring down excess to spotlight a few high-quality items. This was reflected in her home decor and in her fashion choices—she never owned a closetful of clothes but instead rotated her capsule wardrobe of well-made pieces. My grandparents moved a lot, and things that didn't truly matter in life were simply a burden.

One thing that definitely mattered to Grandma was setting her table with the good china for Christmas dinner. After Christmas Eve Mass and a late night with my mom's side of the family, we woke up early the next morning to open gifts and have breakfast in our own house before heading over to Grandma and Grandpa's.

Arriving there was a welcome respite from the hustle and bustle that seemed to fill the air everywhere else. Grandma had a way of making me feel serene. You'd never catch her running around or fussing over arrangements. She always kept the peace of Christmas at the forefront of our celebration, and her attitude made her thoughtful preparations appear effortless. Quality over quantity was her mindset when it came to gift giving too, and toys for her grandchildren were chosen with care. We never had to fill the fridge with piles of leftovers after relishing our Christmas meal. She always made just the right amount of her beef tenderloin, twice-baked potatoes, green beans, buttery cloverleaf rolls and "cranberry salad."

Though she called it a salad, it didn't look like one. A cold, creamy slice of the cranberry concoction sat on the salad plate to the left of our forks on Grandma's beautifully set table. It wasn't a difficult recipe and could wait in the freezer until serving, but the sleek look of each slice exuded Grandma's pared-down sophistication. Even though it was a side dish, its gorgeous shade of pink stole the show and added an unexpected pop all around the table. With the amount of cream and sugar added to offset the tartness of the cranberries, the salad might as well have been a dessert. But that distinction went to Grandma's shortbread cookies.

To this day, I have no idea where the recipe for what I now (more accurately) call Frozen Cranberry Slice originated, but I suppose Grandma got it from one of the few church cookbooks she held on to from move to move. Now that I'm the one hosting Christmas dinner, I always include Grandma's signature dish. We joke that my

CREAMY DELIGHT
Grandma's Frozen Cranberry Slice

80 GUIDEPOSTS

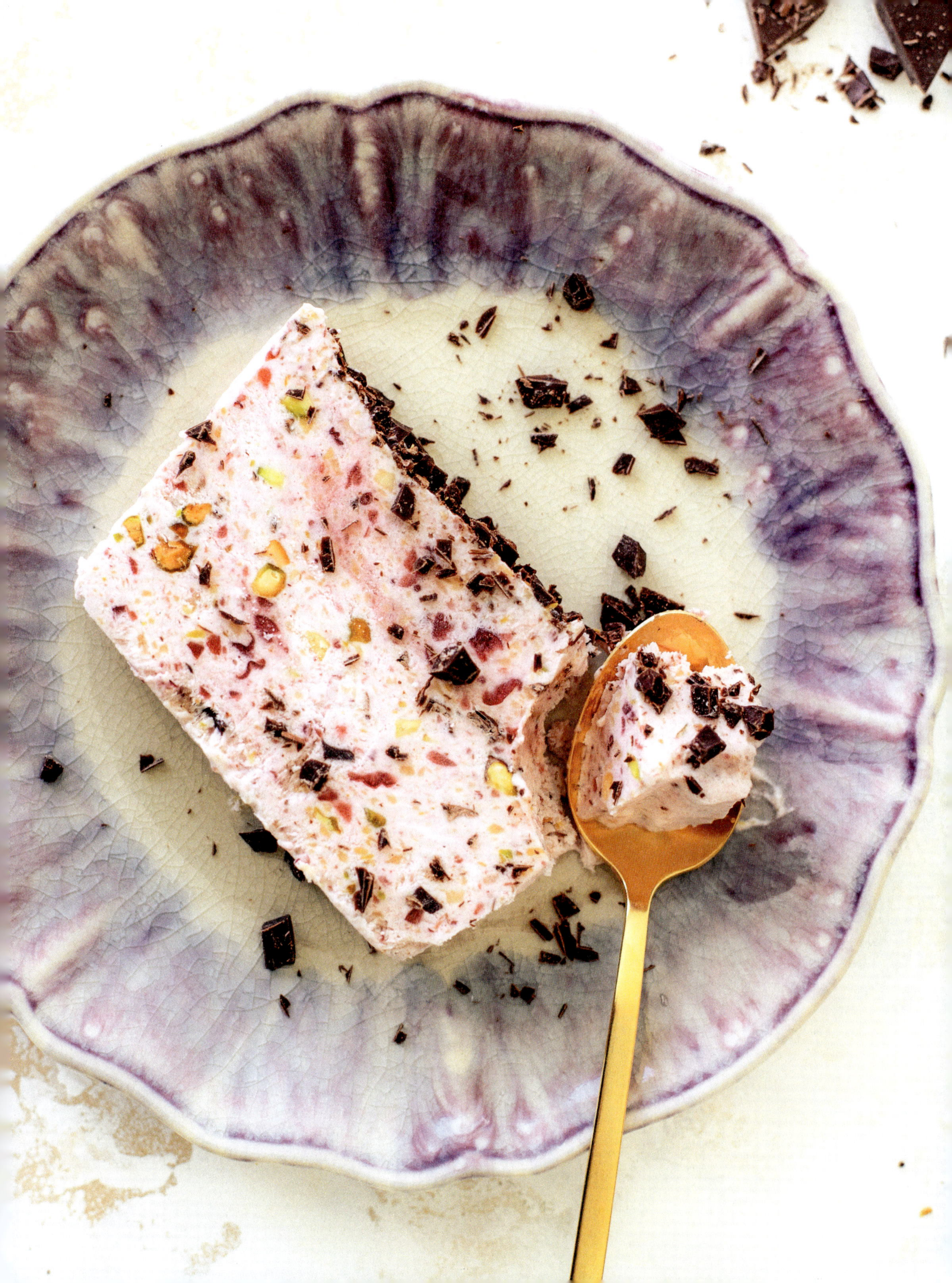

THE JOY OF *cranberries*

Grandma's Frozen Cranberry Slice

- 1 cup heavy cream
- 3 ounces cream cheese, softened
- 2 tablespoons plain Greek yogurt
- 2 tablespoons sugar
- 1 cup chopped fresh pineapple
- 14 ounces whole-berry cranberry sauce
- ½ cup chopped pistachios
- ¼ cup chopped dark chocolate, plus additional for serving

Place a sheet of parchment paper in a 9x5-inch loaf pan. Let the edges hang over, folding them against the sides.

Place the heavy cream in the bowl of a stand mixer. Beat on medium speed until peaks form, 4 to 5 minutes, and the cream is whipped. Set aside.

Place the cream cheese, yogurt and sugar in the bowl of a food processor. Blend until the mixture is smooth and combined. Add the pineapple and pulse a few times until the pineapple is finely chopped. Add the cranberry sauce and pulse a few more times. Transfer the mixture to a bowl. Fold in the pistachios. Fold in the whipped cream until the mixture is lighter in color, fluffy and combined. Fold in the dark chocolate.

Press the mixture into the loaf pan. Cover with plastic wrap and freeze for at least 6 hours, or overnight. Remove from the freezer, and use the parchment sides to lift the mixture from the pan. Use a sharp knife to cut into slices. **Serves** 8.

sister-in-law loves it almost as much as she loves my brother!

I've updated the recipe a bit, adding pistachios and dark chocolate for texture. The little hints of green from the chopped pistachios couldn't be more perfect. Just like Grandma, I make the mixture ahead of time, pour it into a loaf pan lined with parchment paper and put it in the freezer until I'm ready to serve it. For me, that means with dessert. My version is almost marshmallowy, reminiscent of ice cream, but tangy.

Also in honor of Grandma's Christmas dinner, I make sure to break out the fine china, which is not something I do often. But I like to think that her philosophy of holding on to what truly matters in life applies especially to Christmas traditions. I hope that our family meal at Christmas will continue to be something peaceful and beautiful—just the way Grandma always made it for me. ✳

HOLIDAY ELEGANCE
Jessica emulates her grandmother with simple yet sophisticated Christmas dinners.